Endorse

"I've known and worked with John for fifteen years and he is unquestionably one of the foremost experts in helping others find their true work calling. In this book, John walks you step by step in finding that next great position including identifying your ideal job, networking, interviewing, and negotiating the offer. John's five tools of an effective job search have been tried and true for countless executives over the years. If you're looking for a job or thinking about making a transition, this is the book for you."

Will McDade | Retired Executive
CFO/COO - Interstate Batteries
Sr. Vice President - Keurig Dr Pepper

"Over the last twenty years, I've had the opportunity to meet and work with many executives, and without a doubt, John stands out as the best in his field. His passion for helping others, combined with his innate instincts and talents, has played a crucial role in assisting hundreds of executives in securing positions. This book serves as a fantastic resource for executives of all ages who are committed to landing their next big opportunity. It offers valuable advice from someone who has navigated the experience personally and gathered insights from thousands over several decades."

Kenton Kisler
Founder at Executive Connection
Co-founder at Pragmatk

FIFTY,
FAT &
FIRED

JOHN
PATRICK
HUGHES

The Executive's
Guide to Getting
Back Into the C-Suite

FIFTY, FAT & FIRED

LIFEWISE BOOKS

FIFTY, **FAT** & FIRED
The Executive's Guide to Getting Back Into the C-Suite

BY JOHN PATRICK HUGHES

Published by:

LIFEWISE BOOKS
PO BOX 1072
Pinehurst, TX 77362
LifeWiseBooks.com

Headshot by James Edward Photography

To contact the author: johnpatrickhughes.com

Print: 978-1-958820-78-0
Ebook: 978-1-958820-79-7

DEDICATION

I dedicate this book to my wife, Jennifer. She never doubted me as I moved through career transitions despite giving her good cause to do so.

CONTENTS

INTRODUCTION

When I was at a major global firm that was preparing for a cataclysmic restructuring that would eliminate forty percent of the jobs in the headquarters, they issued to everyone a book that used analogies involving cheese to talk about accepting change. I remember reading the book and not getting a darned useful thing out of it. My department was still eliminated, and I was no better prepared to deal with the daunting task of looking for a new role amid the dot-com bubble burst. My peers and I did not deserve that brutal career transition experience. While I cannot change the past, I can help you have a better experience.

So, you've just been fired from your executive-level job and have no other prospects lined up. How will you tell your family? How will you pay your bills, your mortgage, your loans? What are you supposed to do next? Deciding how to move forward in the wake of being fired is overwhelming, and it's difficult to figure out where to start. That's where this book, along with my experience, can help.

Losing a job is one of the most stressful things that can happen to someone. For most of us, it will happen several times in a successful career. The purpose of this book is to hypercharge your job search to be the most effective it can be, thus shortening the painful period of unemployment by landing a role that is a better fit for you moving forward.

In an ideal world, you'll have read this book before your termination. You're the kind of person who saw the not-so-distant dark skies and decided to prepare to weather the storm headed your way. You've built a strong network with other professionals who understand your skills and goals, and they are ready and willing to put your name in front of hiring executives.

If this is you, you can extract maximum benefit from the tools, templates, and processes discussed in the chapters to follow. But even if you're not that kind of person or were caught completely off guard and are already in crisis mode, this book can still help you navigate this turbulent and stressful period and come out the other side of it with a job tailored to your skills, needs, and goals.

A personal philosophy that I live by is that you must create the world you want to live in. At some point, everyone needs help. You never know *when* you will need it. That's why it's important to support others when you can so that when you are in need, you've built up a community ready and willing to help you in return.

In a way, I've written this book to honor that philosophy. By designing a guide for executives who are struggling in their professional lives, I hope to encourage others to build their own support networks and spread further kindness in the cutthroat arena that is the corporate world. This book is born not only out of a personal philosophy but also a professional philosophy consisting of tools and templates I've developed over twenty years through trial and error. I have used these tools in my own job searches, as well as seen their effectiveness in searches conducted by close friends in my network.

I've navigated five major job searches in my career, with varying lengths and degrees of success. I first began to develop these tools when, after eighteen years at premier companies such as IBM* and Coca-Cola*, my position and department were eliminated during a massive restructuring. My first search was a rude awakening, and it took twenty-seven months to land a permanent job. I was introduced to the cold reality of who was a friend to me versus who was a friend to my former role. I knew how to be successful at work, but I didn't know how to be successful at *looking* for work.

The second search took nineteen months, shorter but just as painful, and influenced by a bad economy after the market crash of 2008. The third search took nine months after "parachuting" unemployed into a city where I had zero contacts. The fourth time, I took two months to decide whether I was going to change careers at fifty years old. Once I decided to make the change, it only took two additional months of using these processes I developed to convince others I could move into a new industry and job function.

The final search of my career took only ten weeks, during which I was pursuing two completely different jobs concurrently in different industries. I leveraged these tools and managed to land opportunities in both fields, which gave me the ability to choose which best suited my needs. Now, I'll never have to conduct another job search again. By the time you are reading this book I will be happily retired.

In short, I used these tools to get back on my feet and learned over time how to conduct better, more effective job searches that helped me find roles suiting my specific skills and personal needs. While developing this methodology, I also led networking groups. I coached other professionals one-on-one, which allowed me to refine these processes through their experience as well as my own.

When I started as the chapter leader of a financial networking group in Atlanta in 2002, there were roughly fifty members. By the time I left in 2007, there were about one thousand members. This is not a reflection of my ability as a public speaker but a testament to the real desire professionals had for guidance and community during a difficult time in their lives. My intention for writing this book is not for the sake of vanity but to reach out to this community of professionals and lend a helping hand.

As far as my credentials are concerned, I've made a lot of mistakes in my professional career. I've failed a lot, but I wouldn't go back and change any of my failures. If I hadn't failed as much as I did and then made course corrections, I wouldn't be where I am today. If you don't fail, then you're not living at the edge of your abilities.

The real measure of success is how you recover from failure. This book is dedicated to that recovery process and designed to help you bounce back from professional failure in the most effective way possible.

CHAPTER 1

CENTRAL THEMES

The ideas and templates we will cover in this book all center on the same five themes. These templates, philosophies, and themes come together to form a plan of action designed specifically to help the unemployed executive get back into the C-suite.

PROGRESS, NOT ACTIVITY

When beginning your job search, it is important to know the difference between progress and activity. At first, it may seem counterintuitive because when you're out of work and you're not paying your bills, the hard worker in you is going to say, "You know what, I'm going to put a hundred hours a week into this search." In the panic of losing a job, it feels right to just throw yourself into the search, applying to everything you see in a frenzy. But activity is not the antidote to panic. It's not about how many emails, letters, phone calls, or events; it's about making actual, quantifiable progress.

I learned this the hard way during one of my own job searches. I took all the energy I usually applied to my former job and threw myself into the search. I kept a log of all my activities and recorded every step. I sent out some ungodly number of emails every day, organized phone calls, and went to as many networking meetings as physically possible. I did this for over a year and was no closer to a job than I was on day one. I was mentally and physically exhausted and still not making any money. It was only after a year of doing it wrong that I realized my metric was incorrect. With this discovery, I began to develop proper tools for measuring progress and success.

FOCUS, FOCUS, FOCUS

So, how can you tell the difference between progress and activity? The key is developing clarity about what you want your future role to look like. Once you develop that clarity, you'll gain confidence in your messaging and direction and thus be able to effectively channel your energies into the right people and activities. By the "right" people and activities, I mean those that will actually help you achieve the role you desire. You must decide what your personal vision of future success will be and only engage with people and activities that will get you there. You'll project that clarity to the people you interact with, whether they be recruiters, peers, or new people you meet.

When you have clarity and focus, it leads to confidence in your direction and messaging. When you have clarity, focus, and confidence, the people you interact with will understand where you best fit in. They'll be more willing and likely more able to help you get to where you want to go. In short, clarity for yourself and what you want increases your confidence in your message and direction. Clarity for your audience or network increases their willingness and ability to assist you.

But the idea of focus in the job search isn't only about narrowing your goals, it's also about dedicating yourself to the search and achieving single-minded focus. If you've lost your job and are in a career transition, your one focus in life must be the job search. The period after you've been laid off is not a vacation. Don't be the executive who takes a six-month sabbatical after being laid off and doesn't do any networking within that time. Of course, taking a few weeks to consider what you really want and need in your career is normal and likely necessary. But don't take any longer than four weeks to do so. Reevaluate your career path and use the time to decide on a plan of action for moving forward.

Additionally, don't use this time to suddenly take up projects around the house or decide to coach your kid's soccer team. If the "honey do's" are urgent and you're unable to hire someone else to accomplish them, then by all means, get them done. But if they've been on the back burner for a long time or can easily be done by an outside hire, then leave them be. It can remain on the list for a while longer while you sort out your priorities.

Regarding incremental activities, it's fine if you limit it to a couple of hours a week, as long as that time is not otherwise valuable job search time. Of course, your kids would want you to participate in their activities, but their hierarchy of needs demands that you first focus on regaining an income that will pay for their food and shelter. In short, you must budget your time the same way you budget your money during this period of unemployment. Focusing your time and energy on the search is the only way to ensure that it's a brief blip of pain instead of a years-long stretch of suffering.

CONSISTENT MESSAGING

How does this clarity or focus then manifest itself? It becomes evident in the consistency of your messaging. In order to be consistent in your messaging, you first have to understand what you want to accomplish with your message. What have you made your career about? What have you done professionally? What do you want to accomplish next? Why should people be interested?

At all times during your search, it is important to know the answer to these questions. It is equally important that the answers do not change when you relay them to others, whether it be in conversation, email, social media, or in the way you present yourself physically. When you know the answer to these questions, are you presenting them to others accurately? Do you say the same thing to everyone about yourself, your goals, or your accomplishments? It's as much about the words you choose in conversations as it is about the way you dress and present yourself.

Are you dressing appropriately for a professional of your level? If you show up to a networking event in jeans and a T-shirt, no one will take you seriously. There's a good reason for the old saying, "Dress for the job you want," because it works! You must be consistent in your messaging in all aspects across all platforms: your physical presentation, your conversations, and your LinkedIn® profile. If your message is the same all the time, eventually, it will cut through the white noise of everything else in the job market. People will recognize your name and your message, and it just might land you the role you desire.

For example, many years ago, during one of my job searches, I was in a role in a line of work I didn't particularly care for, but it paid the bills at the time. One day, I got a call out of the blue from a fellow executive whom I'd met in passing through a networking event and whom I hadn't heard from in quite a while. He asked to meet for a coffee to talk about a possible opportunity. When I met with him, he told me, "I've actually asked several of my friends about who would fit this job profile, and four of them came back with your name."

He told me about the role, and I spoke about how I'd approach it. By the end of the conversation, I had landed my ideal job. I was hired on the spot with no resume, no direct networking, and no business card exchange. Such is the ripple effect and the power of consistent messaging; it reaches your entire network, which then relays it outward to others until it comes back to you in the form of a job opportunity.

UNRELENTING DISCIPLINE

There can be no progress or focus without first having unrelenting discipline. When you commit yourself completely to the process and remain disciplined, it becomes easier to maintain your consistent messaging and focus, which eventually leads to progress and results. The job search isn't something you do for a week and then focus on other things for a while and eventually circle back. You must develop an ironclad commitment to the process and be disciplined in every aspect. You must carve out time for the job search; all work, family, and personal activities must flex to accommodate the search.

As much as we'd all like the job search to be brief, you must understand that it is a process that develops in its own time, and you must maintain the patience to see it through. It's not something you can weave in and out of; you must stay the course. It's important to remember that progress has its own pace.

NOT A MENU

When used effectively, these themes and templates work together and empower each other to provide success. It's not a menu to pick and choose from; you must do every step to achieve the desired result. If you do not integrate all these ideas and use the templates, you open yourself up to distractions and self-sabotage. If you pick and choose which elements to favor, you'll end up with generalized activity and not the focused progress that you need.

Now that we understand the underlying themes that power this approach to the executive job search, let's get started.

CHAPTER 2

SHIT HAPPENS

Well, this is it. The worst day of your career. So far. I say "so far" because it's likely to happen again. That's just the way corporate life is. And if you're already at the executive level, then you really shouldn't even be surprised. When it comes to your career, whenever there is a doubt about the safety or stability of your role, then there really is no doubt your job is at risk. If you *have* a worry, then you *should* be worried. It's likely some part of you has recognized one of the warning signs that your job is in danger.

COMMON WARNING SIGNS YOUR JOB IS AT RISK

- your boss/peers almost never accept your point of view on business issues—you feel "out of sync" in most conversations of consequence
- excessive amount of conflict with your boss/peers

- excessive amount of conflict with your direct reports
- you behaved inappropriately at the company event—
  this could be language, rudeness, forceful disagreement
  with company policy, or resistance to change
- your boss behaved inappropriately at a company event
  and scapegoated you—this could be sexual harassment
  or alcohol-related
- your company is past three iterations of the annual
  business plan—major changes are looming
- your company has a major product or business process
  failure—you need not have been the cause to bear the
  brunt of the resulting changes
- your company is losing money at an accelerating rate or
  for a prolonged period
- you are hearing about major initiatives/decisions after
  the fact instead of being a part of the process
- you have a new boss—they may want to bring in people
  they worked with previously
- there is a change in ownership—Private Equity
  Funds are well-known for the quick turnover of
  leadership teams
- you have a "gut feeling" there are forces moving against
  you—this is not about "garden variety" paranoia—
  instinct and pack mentality are rooted in our DNA

So, one or more of these situations happened, and now you've walked into your boss's office, and human resources is there. The most important thing to remember is that you can't change what has happened. There is no use in arguing; it's like trying to change yesterday's newspaper. It's best to calmly accept and do your best to influence tomorrow's headline.

It's understandable to be confused or angry, as there are likely plenty of things running through your mind. But acting on impulse and causing a scene is *never* a good idea. It might be tempting to inform your boss why you always hated them or the company or the job itself, but you need to remember that burning bridges will hurt your chances of finding another role elsewhere. It's best to say as little as possible.

I make this point with a cautionary tale I witnessed. I once knew a business leader who had a strong history of success, ran a solid team, and provided great results in a global consumer products company. Then, the company went through a period of restructuring, and that person's position was eliminated. I remember hearing that they went absolutely ballistic, made a huge scene, and had to be escorted out of the building by the police. All their hard work, success, and influence in the business became useless. Nobody from their former company wanted to associate with them, and they essentially cut off all avenues for obtaining references. I never heard from or about them again.

All of this is to say that as upset as you likely are, maintaining positive connections with your boss and coworkers is more important than your ego or pride. The time for pride has long since passed. Instead, you must employ your Immediate Action Plan to minimize the damage.

FIFTY, **FAT** & FIRED

IMMEDIATE ACTION PLAN

The Immediate Action Plan should be threefold:

    a. take advantage of the "guilt window"

    b. obtain key references

    c. align with your former employer on the "story" of your departure

Guilt Window

During the meeting in which you are being fired, there is the opening of what I call the "guilt window." Your boss is giving you bad news, and odds are they don't enjoy being in this position as the bad guy. They know what this means for you personally and professionally, and they probably wish they could ameliorate the anxiety you're feeling. You have a very short window during that meeting, or perhaps the following day, to take advantage of the guilt they feel for firing you, so be prepared to advocate for yourself and your needs.

The number one thing I tell people to ask for during this window is more severance. Once, I was working at a company going through its fourth replanning cycle for the fiscal year, and my position was eliminated. I hadn't been at the company long, but during the meeting with my boss, I had the presence of mind to ask for an additional month of severance. I also provided reasons for why I felt that I deserved it. My boss said he'd take it into consideration, and the next day, he got back to me and told me it was granted. By having three months of severance instead

18

of two, I extended that cash flow until I secured my next role and had less worries during the job search.

I also recommend asking for an extension of health benefits, a few more weeks before your last day of employment, or even renegotiating the terms of your employment and compensation by offering to come back on a contractual basis for certain projects. As an example, I was in a business development role for a boutique consulting firm when they experienced a significant drop-off in business. The owners understandably had to enact significant cost-cutting measures, including eliminating my role. I was able to successfully argue that they needed business development to stabilize the firm, and I was willing to drastically change the composition of my compensation program to be very highly dependent on new sales.

This allowed the company to keep a new sales pipeline and for me to keep a job. A year later, we were able to restructure the compensation back to a more balanced level of risk and reward. The reality is that you never know when your job will end, so always have in mind what is the most valuable and achievable concession to request in case your termination occurs today. This will allow you to somewhat mitigate the stress of the coming months.

Key References

After you've sorted out what gets through the guilt window, the next step is lining up key references for LinkedIn and future interviews. If you're a C-level executive, have people from your former company as references, whether it's the CEO, a board member, or another C-level peer. The funny thing about references is that most people aren't quite sure what to say. The best way to ensure you get a reference letter that best speaks to your abilities is by writing the draft yourself. Therefore, make sure it focuses on a particular aspect of your value proposition you want to push forward to potential employers. Your reference can then edit the draft into their own voice and be assured they're sending a letter that best represents you.

If you were the controller of the firm and your position is going away, then you'll want the CFO to speak to your reliability and handling of the monthly closing process. If your reference is a CEO or board member, you'll want them to talk about how comprehensive and insightful the board presentation decks were that you had prepared for them. If it's a C-suite peer, have them speak to how you and the team you led were always reliable to help and provide accurate information for them when requested. The skills you mention in the draft should correlate with the unique position and relationship you had with the reference.

Aligning the Story of Your Departure

The third and final part of the conversation with your now-former boss should be aligning the story of your departure. The objective, of course, is a win-win solution—a story that makes both you and your employer look good. If it were divorce, it'd be a no-fault one. The corporate world is very small, especially at senior levels. Therefore, it's important to get along not just for today but tomorrow as well.

Start the conversation with your former boss like this: "Look, what's happened has happened. We both need to move forward and prosper personally and professionally. I want to feel good about this company, its people, and my efforts to create value here, and I want the company to feel the same about me. So, let's figure out how to ensure everybody looks good coming out of this."

This part of the conversation doesn't necessarily need to happen while you're still in the meeting, but you do need to plant seeds for it during your termination meeting. The main priority is taking advantage of the guilt window, but you can set up the conversation to align your stories simultaneously.

It's simple to say: "I want to reflect on this over the next couple of days, then circle back to set up a call. Let's talk about [what you asked for in the guilt window] and how we make sure everybody looks good going forward." Ideally, during the termination meeting, you will agree to a specific day and time for a follow-up discussion. Given the level of anxiety and guilt your boss is feeling, this should be easy to schedule.

For example, a friend of mine was once in transition and eager to get back to work. He had an opportunity to work for a start-up that wanted a finance leader. It was in the industry he wanted to be in, but I didn't think that it was a good fit for him. He took it anyway, but in a matter of about three weeks, he realized it was a poor match. Soon thereafter, the company felt the same way and decided to part ways with him.

When I spoke to him, I encouraged him to reach out to the owner of the startup business and to lay out a scenario in which he would speak highly of the firm, and they would speak highly of him. He would say that he was glad to have joined the firm when he did and happy to have quickly solved some significant issues in a short time that positioned them for growth. But the reality is that they didn't need the horsepower and the expense of a CFO at the time, so it was better that he separated from the company so they could keep their expenses in line and continue to grow.

Even though he had accepted a permanent role, both he and the company agreed they would consider it a consulting assignment. Therefore, it wouldn't look like a mistake, it would look like a mission accomplished. That's the goal of aligning your stories: a win-win solution allowing you to speak highly of your former company and them to speak highly of you.

No doubt, this has been a brutal day. But you would do well to put this day into the perspective of failure vs. failed. Failure is an activity. Failed is a terminal state. Losing a job is a failure. It is an integral part of an executive's career life cycle of:

> *Success* over time leads to failure…
>
> *Failure* is the mother of course corrections…
>
> *Course Corrections* fuel an effective job search…

Effective Job Search leads to a new job that is an ideal fit for your needs now and into the future…

Ideal New Job positions you for success…

Success leads you to the next iteration of the cycle.

I have experienced career failures several times, and each time, it has led to course corrections, personal growth, and, eventually, to incremental success. As painful as they were at the time, I would not forgo any of the failures because doing so would have led me on a different path or potentially a career dead-end and precluded me from writing this book and concluding my career on a happy note.

As long as you are engaging in course corrections and conducting a robust job search, you will eventually secure a new role that is a better fit for your current and future needs. However, if you *do not* make the corrections or *do not* conduct an effective job search (as we will detail later in this book), you will have condemned yourself to a series of short employment periods and extended job searches and will have failed as a professional.

Unfortunately, after the meeting and follow-ups with your former boss, the tough conversations aren't over. The next step is perhaps even more difficult—talking to your family.

CHAPTER 3

TOUGH CONVERSATIONS WITH FAMILY

The conversation after you arrive home from being fired is often harder than the one you just had with your former employer. There are people at home who look up to you and rely on you, and losing your job impacts not only you but your family as well. Therefore, you will need to have a series of uncomfortable but necessary conversations with your family.

First, you must build a new family budget. Every household lives by different means, but during this period between jobs, you're all going to have to exist on a much leaner budget. Since you should expect to be in a career transition from six to twelve months, it is essential you implement the changes right away. You'll have to reevaluate what you consider "must-haves" against your current financial state. It might be helpful to take a "zero-based budgeting" approach and examine each type of expense to determine whether to include it going forward and what actions can be taken to reduce it or manage cost increases in the future.

BUDGET REDUCTION/EVALUATION CONVERSATION

Here are some talking points:

Mortgage—This must be accepted as is in the short term. Depending on current interest rates, there may be an opportunity to refinance the home at a lower interest rate. However, unless your co-signer has an appropriate-level income, the bank may be unwilling to approve a revised loan.

Rent—This must also be accepted in the short term. By continuing to pay your rent on time, you may be able to convince the landlord to refrain from rent increases while you are unemployed.

Electricity / Gas Utility—Take control of the thermostat and maintain settings that reduce energy costs. Needing to wear an incremental layer of clothing during the winter and running room fans in the summer will be an adjustment but an impactful one to your budget.

College Tuition—The responsibility lies with the student. Naturally, parents want to provide for all their children's needs, but nowadays, college tuition costs can be the largest line item in a family's budget. As college marks the transition from teenager to adult, now can be the time for them to learn the importance of cost-benefit tradeoff analysis. The student will become responsible for securing loans to cover the cost of tuition and room and board. Help your children work through the decision process of whether they take responsibility for the school loans or defer their education a year by seeking out an internship for their "gap year." This may seem harsh, but such a large chunk of money isn't trivial. It requires deep consideration as to whether it belongs in your slimmed-down budget.

Outside Entertainment—They will be off-limits for now. Movies, concerts, and sporting events are luxuries you can look forward to resuming after you have returned to work. If you are a member of a country club, inquire if it is possible to freeze your membership during your career transition.

Cable & Internet—These options are more opportunities to reduce expenses. Since you will not be engaging in external entertainment, this will be a viable substitute for the family and can still reduce expenses. If you have not yet "cut the cable," now is the time to switch to a cost-effective collection of streaming services. If you have already switched to streaming, take an inventory of the various costs and coverages. Reduce your costs as much as possible by eliminating redundant services, and for the premium movie services, suspend subscriptions for months at a time as you oscillate between them. Given that their video libraries retain titles for viewing for many months, family members will be able to view their favorite movies and shows at some point.

FIFTY, **FAT &** FIRED

Outside Dining—This should be limited to the occasional splurge for a fast-food meal. There will be time to celebrate over a fine dinner after you land your next role.

Groceries—There are a myriad of ways to reduce food costs. Eliminate delivery fees by doing your own shopping. Base your weekly menu on what the grocery stores have on sale that week. Switch to less expensive cuts of protein. Replace expensive national brands with private labels and store brands. Eschew prepared foods by buying the base ingredients and making the food yourself. Finally, switch to grocery stores that offer the best value and shop at multiple stores to "cherry-pick" the lowest prices.

Vacations—Cost containment opportunities are situational. If you've had a vacation planned for a long time, try to get a refund, if possible. If it's not possible, then take it. You probably need it now more than ever. However, don't plan any new ones.

It's also time to consider alternative sources of revenue. If it's possible to sell one of the household cars, do so. Assess the needs and expenses of a vacation home and whether it's worth it to sell. If selling it is not an option, what about turning it into a full-time rental to raise some income? Given that you will not be taking vacations for a while, adult toys like motorcycles, boats, snowmobiles, etc., are likely not to be used soon, so they should be assessed for resale value. Any extraneous items with a decent cash value should be sold so you can build up a cash hoard to get you through the coming months.

INDIVIDUAL CONVERSATIONS

Regarding the actual conversation with your family, help your family understand that these cutbacks are necessary to ensure an easier future for all of you and that everyone has a part to play. For your part, you'll be dedicating your time and energy to finding a new job as quickly as possible. For their part, they need to get on board with the new budget and do their best to not add to the mental or financial stress in the coming months. In fact, anything they can do to alleviate stress is welcome. This could include other members of the household getting a job if they don't have one or perhaps picking up an additional source of income.

The conversation will vary by family member. With your spouse or partner, the focus should be on the importance of putting on a "brave face" to the rest of the family that this will all work out in the end. You will want to tell your partner that you will keep them informed of your progress and seek their counsel. This will likely be a very stressful time for them as well, so providing an avenue for them to contribute will be very constructive.

For older children (high school and older), you will want to emphasize that career transition is a normal phase in one's career (one they will likely also encounter) and that you expect it to lead to a better role. Let them know this is such a common occurrence and has likely happened to some of their friends' parents, and they successfully moved through the transition. If your new family budget includes transferring the cost of college onto the student, you will want to have a deep conversation

FIFTY, **FAT** & FIRED

regarding the tradeoffs of taking on student loans, transferring to a less expensive college, or pursuing an internship or a meaningful gap year.

For younger children, you will want to keep them in the dark as much as possible about your career transition. Let them know that just as they move from one school to another as they get older, it is time for you to move on to a new company. Tell them that during this period, you are looking forward to being around them more often and hopefully attending more of their sporting events and activities.

It's important that everyone in the family, including yourself, understands that the only way out of this hard time is through mutual support and flexibility. The family must be on the same page and work together as a team to overcome any obstacles headed their way.

To help you understand the importance of this issue, I would like to share a quick story. Several years ago, a good friend of mine who lived on the East Coast took a controller role in the Midwest that required him to work from the Midwest headquarters for three out of four weeks. He was very successful in his role, and in time, he was promoted to CFO. When the job came to an end (they always do), he had a year of severance to fund his transition.

During his extensive time in the Midwest, which had a thriving job market, he built up a network of professional connections. He now had the option of looking for his next role in the thriving job market he had worked in the last few years or returning

30

to his host city, which I like to refer to as "where good careers go to die."

Naturally, his family wanted to stay in their home and for him to work locally. The family continued to spend money as they always had, as he worked extremely diligently to find a role in a city with scant opportunities. A year later, he still had no income and no job prospects. It has been a hardscrabble ever since.

CHAPTER 4

GETTING YOUR MIND AND BODY RIGHT

FIRST IMPRESSION PREPARATION

Now that you have updated the family for the path ahead, it is time to prepare yourself for the strenuous and ultimately rewarding personal growth phase. The months leading up to the loss of a job are very stressful and can take a toll on your health. It's likely that in the past months, work has taken up your entire focus, and your own needs have largely been ignored. Lack of sleep and exercise, as well as poor eating, lead to mental and physical deterioration that is exacerbated in the period after losing a job. It's, therefore, necessary to look in the mirror and examine yourself. Is this the visage of someone who is likely to be hired?

This book is called *Fifty, Fat, and Fired* for a reason. At this point in your life, you're probably no longer at your peak physical shape, and now, you're not in peak professional shape, either. It's time for you, your partner, and your family to conduct a brutally honest assessment of your physical and mental state.

PHYSICAL STATE

Appearances very much matter when you are conducting a job search because you are about to meet many new people who will be forming opinions based on their first impression of you, which starts before you even begin to speak. There have been studies done claiming interviewers make their decision within the first few minutes. The reality is that your appearance plays a significant role in projecting your competence and professionalism to people meeting you for the first time. You must stop and ask: "What does my appearance say about me?" Let's do a head-to-toe assessment:

Hair—Are you showing more gray than you would like? Maybe touch it up a bit, so as not to look as old as you may feel. This comment applies to men as well. Don't feel awkward about it. Most men's hair salons offer a coloring service, and the haircare aisles are filled with options. Showing less gray will provide a boost to the energy level and confidence you project.

Glasses—The truth is that by the time one has reached the executive level, almost everyone will have vision impairment to some degree. If you prefer glasses over contact lenses, ensure the frames are stylish and contemporary.

Facial Hair—I have a friend with whom I worked with many years ago, and he had this great, sophisticated white beard. But when he was conducting a job search, he would always shave it. So, anytime I got a video call from him and saw his clean-shaven face, I knew exactly what the call was about. Although his beard was a defining characteristic, he understood that being clean-shaven conveyed a younger, more professional image when looking for his next role. If you elect to retain the facial hair, ensure it is well groomed. I have a teammate who has a "Hercule Poirot" style mustache. It is a work of art and is central to his personal style. I would never ask him to shave it.

Dress Shirts—I'm always amazed when I see in-transition people at networking events wearing a golf shirt as if they are on a quick run to the grocery store or are wearing dress shirts that make them look like a sausage casing. If your professional clothing doesn't fit, it's not doing you any favors. In fact, it may be harming your chances of landing your next role. Invest in new clothing—three mid-to-high quality button-down dress shirts measured to fit and flatter you. Skip the monogramming and put the money into a higher-quality shirt fabric. Don't buy a shirt that has a 34/35 sleeve when your arm is a size 35. Go up half a size on the neck. Buy them all in white—it goes with everything, and if they're the same color, nobody will notice you have a short rotation of shirts.

Dress Slacks and Sports Coats—It will be too expensive to buy three whole new outfits, but take your existing clothes to a dry cleaner or tailor to see if it's possible for them to alter them to fit you better.

Accessories—This is your opportunity to accent your appearance with items that reflect your personal style or history, and that can be an introduction to a short and mildly interesting story. For instance, a wristwatch or heirloom jewelry you inherited from a grandparent. On the contrary, a Fitbit® or a digital watch is not helping your cause. I had a teammate who always wore a lapel pin of the presidential seal from his days as a senior government official. I prefer a sterling silver shamrock-shaped lapel pin given to me by my nephew, who works in the Irish Consulate and reminds me of my time in graduate school in Dublin. You are best advised to avoid items with a political or social message. The intent is for your accessories to be interesting, not controversial.

Shoes—What kind of shape are they in? Can they be fixed with a good shine? If not, it may be time to invest in a new pair. If your shoes look old and out of place with the rest of your clothing, people will take notice of this discrepancy.

The final aspect of your appearance that requires assessment is your weight. As I said earlier, the run-up to the loss of a job is very stressful and often results in being overweight due to neglected physical needs. Don't kid yourself into thinking you do not need to lose some weight to project a healthier and more vibrant first impression. Here is a simple test: go to the back of your closet and try on an outfit you have not worn in ten years. These pants were not called "skinny jeans" when you bought them. They no longer fit because you are no longer skinny!

Figure out what exercise works best for you for both weight loss and stress reduction. Personally, I walk four miles every morning at a brisk pace. I find that it helps me destress and is a great cardio exercise. I also use it as a chance to ruminate and gain a fresh perspective on any complex issues of the day. Other examples of exercise could include weightlifting, running, or other activities that can be accomplished in only an hour or less daily.

However, don't get involved in time-consuming activities such as golf, which take up the better hours of daylight. That time is better spent on the actual job search. Regardless of your exercise program, set a weight loss goal and make it happen. At this point, so much is out of control, so take control of this challenge and relish your success. This positive energy will be an important asset on the other side of your preparation—the mental side.

MENTAL STATE

When taking stock of your mental health during this time, you will benefit by adopting a "nudist" approach to your job search. Relieve yourself of the burden of pride or embarrassment. You are out of work, and you need to benefit from the kindness of others. You need to know how to recognize when you need help, as well as how to ask for it. Do not be reluctant to share information on your career path and future aspirations, including compensation. By being open and honest with people, you will engender trust and advocacy from others to help you.

You also must prepare for a job search that will be a marathon of sprints. Everyone wants their job search to be brief, but the reality is that you will likely be out of work for six to twelve months. I've had longer searches as well as shorter ones, but it's best to plan for the worst. You must prepare yourself to have the physical and mental strength to endure this period, no matter how long it lasts. There will be times when you have a load of activity, and you're sprinting ahead, and you will also have periods where you have zero current opportunities, and it feels like you're stuck. Stay focused to sustain yourself on this long run.

Here are several maxims that are essential to sustaining a successful job search:

- *Focus on "What Next?" Instead of "What Happened?"*—Your search needs to maintain a focus on actions you can take to influence your future instead of dwelling on what happened. You do need to reflect on what has just happened so it can inform your future course corrections, but do not belabor bad luck or mistakes.
- *Always Respond, But Never React*—There is no doubt some people and some occurrences are going to really disappoint you during your search. Be prepared to be profoundly disappointed so you can resist the temptation to express your dissatisfaction or anger. It won't change what happened but will damage your relationship with those people who witnessed it directly and indirectly.
- *Positivity*—In my experience, emanating a positive attitude tends to attract other people with a positive attitude. Think of it this way: how many movies have you enjoyed watching a plucky underdog strive through

challenges and then shared their joy when they were
ultimately successful? Do you have the same reaction to
someone drowning in despair during their job search?
No, of course not. You back away so you do not get
sucked into their vortex.

- *Have Faith*—Unfortunately, some people, especially
  when the search process is taking longer than they
  expected, start to show their worst qualities as despair
  and panic erode their confidence. The key to forestalling
  this decline in their candidacy is faith. *Faith* in their
  ability to replicate in their next role the millions of
  dollars of value creation they delivered in their prior
  roles. *Faith* in the goodness of others to provide
  them much needed assistance during their search.
  Faith that they are leveraging an effective system of
  templates, processes, and behaviors to reach their next
  executive role, which will be an ideal match for their
  current needs.

Hopefully, these foundational chapters have provided you with a
starting point to embark on a new and highly effective approach
to your job search. So far, we've covered the central themes,
surviving your worst day, sharing the news with your family,
and getting your mind and body right for the challenge ahead of
you. While this may seem like rudimentary information, these
are all necessary steps to position yourself for success before fully
launching into the job search.

Whether or not you are going to be ultimately successful is dependent upon your ability to leverage the tools, templates, and processes detailed in the following chapters.

CHAPTER 5

THE FIVE TOOLS OF AN EFFECTIVE JOB SEARCH

This chapter details the templates at the core of this highly effective and time-efficient process for an executive's job search. The intent is to explain the templates in detail and how to best use them as part of an interdependent system.

TOOL A: THE IDEAL JOB PROFILE

The first and most integral template is the Ideal Job Profile. The Ideal Job Profile, or "IJP" for short, is a description of the role that best meets your professional needs tomorrow. It is the first step and cornerstone of a successful job search because how can you expect to land the right role if you do not know what it looks like? You must start with the end in mind.

So, why is the IJP not just a description of your current role? The reality is that as we move through life, what we need and desire from our professional roles continues to evolve. The in-transition period between roles is an ideal time to take stock of what type of job will best fit your current set of needs. Your IJP continues to evolve for a range of factors:

- *Financial*—Your spouse or partner may have an income that covers a substantial portion of your financial needs. Or, you have sizable private school or college tuition obligations on the horizon or, conversely, now behind you. You could also be facing significant healthcare expenses or that financial drain just ended.

- *Work and Life Balance*—Are your children at an age where they need more of your time, or are they now past that phase? In a similar vein, you may have aging parents who need more of your time or who have recently passed. High travel may have impacted your relationship with your spouse, or you are now on your own. Finally, you may want to move to another part of the country to be close to family members or because you intend to retire there in a few years.

- *Psychological and Emotional*—You continue to aspire to achieve a certain job title, or you are bored with your industry/functional area or level of responsibility and/or crave a change.

- *Economic*—Your current industry or part of the country is in decline.

The process of determining your IJP is an open-ended questionnaire of approximately sixteen questions that cover the most relevant aspects of an executive's role. The questions are grouped into several categories.

Visit **JohnPatrickHughes.com/templates**
for your free download of all templates.

JOB ELEMENTS

These questions explore the core aspects of the role and include:

Title—What title are you seeking? CXO, EVP, SVP, VP, Director? Or is the title not important to you?

Location—Where is the position located? If not in your current city, are you open to working in a hybrid or remote role?

Travel—What is the travel component of the role? How often will you be out of town, and where will you be traveling? International travel tends to be a big plus or a big negative. Work travel itself is disruptive, can be stimulating, and will impact work and life balance, so one would do well to ensure you have clarity on your preferences.

Span of Control—Is another key consideration and is manifested in a variety of dimensions:

Geography—Is the role regional, national, or global?

Organizational—What functions report to this role?

People—Is the role an individual contributor, or will it lead a small team or maybe a large team?

COMPENSATION ELEMENTS AND VALUES

These questions explore the financial aspects of your ideal role and include:

Base Salary—This will reflect both your compensation needs and market pricing for the role and geography. Roles in high-cost cities will pay somewhat more than in more affordable locations. Think in terms of a range with the higher end being fifty percent above the bottom of the range and list the higher value first. It is important that you are willing to accept a role that offers compensation at the bottom of your range; otherwise, raise it to a level you would accept without regret.

Bonus—You need to determine your target bonus percentage, how it is calculated, the degree to which it is discretionary and by whom, and the payout ratios in recent years. Depending upon the ownership structure (family-owned, private equity-backed, employee stock ownership plan (ESOP), public company, or non-profit), what is "normal" will vary greatly.

Equity—You are more likely to have an opportunity for equity in private-equity-backed firms for a handful of CXO roles, but some private firms have a "shadow equity" program. ESOP contributions are one form of shadow equity, but companies can craft their own version as well. If you are participating in an equity program, anticipate a smaller bonus program.

Other Benefits—Usually, this is the lowest priority and comes in a variety of forms. It could include an Executive Healthcare Plan (assuming traditional HMO medical/dental/vision plans are offered to all employees), memberships to professional associations, Country Club membership and/or annual dues, car allowance or company vehicle, or a travel and entertainment budget.

ORGANIZATION AND STRUCTURE

These questions pertain to the day-to-day aspects of the role and include:

Who would you report to in this role? I have seen general counsel roles report to both CEOs and COOs. Do you care?

What is your level of autonomy? Will your boss be heavily involved in reviewing your key decisions and/or day-to-day leadership decisions, or will they be hands-off after your initial period in the role? The source of additional decision-making involvement also includes the private equity representatives on the board of directors. Do you care?

With whom will you have regular interaction? Do you feel it is important to have direct meetings with the board of directors, other functional leaders, or external groups such as investors, banks, and regulatory agencies?

What departments will directly report to this role? For example, if you are seeking the role of Chief Marketing Officer, do you care if the sales function is within your purview as well? If you are looking at Chief Financial Officer roles in a public company, is it important to you that investor relations report to you?

Do you have a strong preference on the degree of financial stability of the company? Still, others seek out firms setting out on a mergers and acquisitions binge for the thrill of the transaction. Finally, there are those folks who enjoy a more steady-state environment while driving measured growth. They are all valid options; the key is to be honest with yourself as to which category is best for your needs going forward.

Is there a particular life cycle stage that fits you best? Some leaders prefer start-ups for their wide range of responsibilities. Some people thrive on turnaround situations because they seek the freedom to implement significant change rapidly. There are still others that thrive in a fairly steady state or low growth environment that provides an opportunity to use their skills to increase profitability through operational excellence and profit improvement initiatives. What type are you?

CAREER PATH

Naturally, one's primary focus is the job at hand, but do not lose sight of how this job fits into your life-long career plan.

Does this job serve as a logical stepping stone on the career path you have outlined for yourself? If your ultimate career goal is to be CFO and you are currently interviewing for the Controller position, you would want to understand how long the CFO intends to remain and would you be part of the succession plan.

What is your expectation for the duration of the role, and how does that align with your plans? If you want to work two more years and the private equity backer intends to sell the company in a similar timeframe, then it could be a good match. However, if you are looking for a role where you can spend at least five years in and the company has a history of turning over the leadership team every eighteen months, you will probably want to avoid this company.

HOW TO USE IT

STEP ONE is spending no more than two hours completing the questionnaire. If it is taking you longer, then you are overthinking it and trying to guess the "right answers." You must approach this from the perspective of imagining the role that would fit your needs and wants of today. It must be done in a vacuum and not influenced by your previous roles or a current job opportunity.

STEP TWO is sharing the IJP with your spouse or partner and asking for their feedback. If you do not have one, then grown children or close friends who know you well will do. As you know, they love to "call bullshit" on us. They will respond with feedback such as:

> *You always said that you did not want XXX responsibilities in your next role.*

> *You often remarked how much you enjoyed XXX aspect of your prior role (or the role before that one).*

> *Do you really want to work in another start-up/turnaround since the stress really seemed to be getting to you?*

> *Are you going to be happy in a role that is smaller than your prior one?*

> *Haven't you been saying that you wanted a fresh start in your role/job level/industry?*

By incorporating this feedback into your IJP, you will have an accurate picture of the attributes of a role that ideally suits your needs and wants of tomorrow.

STEP THREE is to truly embrace this version of the IJP as your next career goal and mentally release yourself from your adherence to prior job or career goals. You must do this to have the focus and consistency required for a successful job search. This newfound knowledge is empowering. Since it accurately addresses your needs, you will naturally be able to speak with conviction as to why a certain type of role is a great fit for you and why you are a great fit for a particular company. This will greatly enhance your networking proficiency, which we will discuss later in the book.

In my own experience, achieving the VP level in my function within a large firm was a long-held goal. I finally achieved it and then some as I was part of the executive leadership team, designated as the successor to the CXO, had my own parking space, and was enrolled in its long-term incentive plan for executives. I moved cross-country to a small market for this role. After only a couple of months, the private equity backer of the firm merged us into another firm and completely wiped out the leadership team. I was grateful to achieve my career-long goal, but I would not waste precious time and energy trying to recreate the same role in a small labor market.

Understanding that leadership roles come and go with all too much frequency, I reset my IJP to live and work in a large, industry-diverse market and to focus on interim roles, so I moved on speculation to a thriving part of the country in which I had no contacts. Given that I had just had a short stint in my prior "permanent role" and that no one knew me, and I had zero frame of reference to identify and evaluate the companies and the opportunities in the new market, it made sense for me to focus on interim roles. This provided a lower barrier to entry, which would allow me the opportunity to build my reputation locally and deepen my understanding of the particular companies and roles that would be a good fit for me long-term while maintaining a cash flow that would allow me to bide my time.

After a couple of years of rewarding interim leadership roles, my IJP informed me it was time to leave my twenty-five-plus years of functional work and transition into management consulting. At age fifty-two, I was able to make the stark career transition from leading a functional team nationally to being a junior consultant.

In time, the consulting firm asked me to move into a business development role for the firm. This necessitated weekly travel to different cities. At first, it was a fun and stimulating challenge. After a couple of years of traveling, for family reasons, I need to "get off the road." In the process of selecting a new firm, I critically analyzed my own value proposition and that of potential firms to identify in which cases my "one" plus their "one" equaled "three." This enabled me to identify the best opportunity to transition to a business development role in a professional services firm and achieve the highest level of success in my entire career.

STEP FOUR is to "sanity check" your IJP for market acceptance. There are three types of IJP, and these are the implications of each:

Expectational—Your current IJP closely mirrors your most recent role or the previous one. For instance, say you spent the last five years as the VP of Marketing of a five-hundred-million-dollar consumer packaged goods company, and you are seeking the same role and industry in your next job. Changes in geographic location, sales level within fifty percent, differing work travel profiles, and differing work and life balances can all fall within the expectational category. This classification is quite common for leaders in their fifties and sixties.

Aspirational—Your current IJP reflects that you are looking to either take the next logical step upward in your current career track or you are seeking to make the jump into a different function or significantly different role or industry. An example of the former is a Controller in a three-hundred-million-dollar revenue manufacturing firm with domestic-only operations seeking to "graduate" up to a Controller/Chief Accounting Officer role in a one-billion-dollar manufacturer with global operations.

An alternative "graduation" target for this candidate could be a Chief Financial Officer role in a three-hundred to five-hundred-million-dollar manufacturing firm with domestic-only operations. Looking at it from a scope of duties perspective, it could be a VP of Sales targeting a VP of Sales & Marketing role for a similar size company and industry. An example of changing career tracks would be a functional leader trying to transition to a professional services firm targeting their prior function. The degree of difficulty is dependent upon the depth and quality of your functional skills, as well as your competence in business development. This classification is quite common for leaders in their forties and fifties looking for the next logical functional "graduation" and for people in their fifties changing careers.

Delusional—Your IJP may reflect what will truly make you most happy in your next role, but it is highly unlikely you can make that leap forward from your current career location. This is the most difficult to diagnose, yet it is most critical to do so because it would necessitate that you revisit your IJP to develop one that is expectational or aspirational in nature.

Several factors can result in a delusional IJP:

- *Job Scope/Company Dimensions*—You seek to move up to a company size that is a multiple of your current one and/or greatly increase your scope of activities. An example is a Chief Financial Officer in a two-hundred-million-dollar revenue, family-owned, consumer packaged goods company, and you are pursuing CFO roles at a one-billion-dollar, publicly traded company with global operations. You will not be competitive with the many candidates with current or prior experience that is much closer than you to the job specifications of the global role.

- *Geography*—The industry you are targeting is scarce in the location you are targeting. If you are a petrochemical engineer, looking for a role in Southern California is not likely to be productive.

- *Industry*—The industry you target is in steep decline, at least in your current geography. Alternatively, you may be targeting to enter an industry with a significant technical knowledge barrier, such as healthcare or natural resources.

- *Economic*—The current economic conditions are causing a slowdown in job rotation as people "hunker down" in their current roles regardless of their level of job satisfaction, and leaders in career transition are "dropping down" into lesser roles to secure work. Their wealth of experience will overwhelm any candidates attempting to make an aspirational career transition. Hopefully, this case in point will illuminate the challenge and appropriate response.

After several years as the Finance Leader of a three-hundred-million-dollar business unit with over fifty locations in the Southeast, I yearned to return to Atlanta and find a role as the Chief Financial Officer of a one-hundred to one-hundred-fifty-million-dollar firm. I was indifferent regarding whether it was a stand-alone company or a subsidiary of a much larger firm. At the time, I had a very strong network in Atlanta, as I had helped many people successfully navigate their career transitions. However, a couple of weeks after I returned, the stock market crashed, and we were at the beginning of the great recession.

Job opportunities dried up due to downsizing, people "hunkering down" in the roles they currently had, and in-transition candidates "dropping down" to lesser roles so that they could wait out the economic slowdown. Regardless of the challenging environment, every six months, I managed to be a finalist in a role I coveted. Each time, I failed to land the role. One would like to think that I finished second each time, but we all know that is not true. Besides, finishing second in a job search is as helpful as second place in a game of live grenade toss.

After the third time, I consulted with my power group (we will cover this topic later in the book). Their blunt and painfully accurate assessment was that I was going deep in the interview process due to my strong work history that equipped me with a "higher ceiling" but a "lower floor" than other candidates because I had not yet proven myself in a standalone CFO role. However, as there were several candidates with prior stand-alone CFO experience, their "higher floor" yet "lower ceiling" made them a safer candidate in the current environment.

As a result, my normally aspirational IJP was, in reality, delusional due to economic and local market factors. In response, I changed my IJP to pursue leading strategic and financial analysis teams and expanded my geographic area of pursuit. A month later, I interviewed for a Director of Financial Planning role. After interviewing, they upgraded it to the VP of Strategic & Financial Planning role and included me in the executive leadership team!

Given that having a delusional IJP will completely derail one's job search, it is paramount that you are able to identify when you are on a path to nowhere. Some of the telltale signs include:

- lack of success in your networking meetings resulting in incremental introductions closer to your targeted companies
- consistently being "screened out" at the first phase of job interviews
- utilizing LinkedIn to conduct an objective comparison of your qualifications and experiences to several people currently in the type of role you seek and conclude that there is a sizable gap you cannot bridge

STEP FIVE is to "get the word out" by consistently incorporating your IJP in every communication format and interaction. This manifests in a variety of ways:

Clearly and concisely communicate the IJP in your Marketing Document (which we will explain in detail in the next chapter) and replicate the messaging in your Marketing Document, in your resume, and LinkedIn profile as well. The key message should also be featured on your business card.

Share your IJP with the Retained Recruiters who work with the type of companies you are targeting. Some people wrongly feel this is revealing too much information and, therefore, reducing any negotiation leverage you may have. The reality is that you are communicating to the Retained Recruiter in terms of what types of roles are the best fit for you, using the same type of information they normally acquire when they are securing recruiting assignments. This will enable the recruiter to engage with you on job opportunities with a strong promise of a solid match. Also, share the IJP with everyone you meet in your networking efforts.

Time in a job search is a precious commodity. If you are conducting a search while you are working, you would be hard-pressed to dedicate more than five hours a week to it. If you are in a career transition, every hour you are incurring expenses but not making any money to pay for them. Therefore, it is essential that you focus your time on activities and opportunities most likely to help you progress toward your IJP.

The IJP is the perfect tool to use as a scorecard to evaluate job opportunities. Roles that "check the box" for eight of the sixteen criteria are not likely to meet your needs, so discard them. Roles that meet twelve of the sixteen criteria are worthy of a quick discussion with the source of the lead to determine the probability of "getting to yes" on the four open criteria. At this time, you will also want to evaluate the relative importance of the various criteria to determine how much time and energy you should put into this pursuit. Roles that meet fourteen or more of your criteria should become your primary focus. Clear your calendar to maintain flexibility to respond to the interview process for these opportunities and use your network to develop insight and connections to the key people at the target company.

An example of this is my last job search. At the start of my search, I sent out notes to fifty-five key contacts to let them know my IJP. Over the next two weeks, I worked fifty hours per week corresponding with these contacts and their direct friends, yielding three job leads that scored highly on my IJP scorecard. I then spent only fifteen hours a week for the next eight weeks going through the interview process for these opportunities and quickly vetting other opportunities that arose. I did not chase low to medium-scoring opportunities, so I could maintain my availability to interview for the high-scoring opportunities when they were ready to move forward in the process. As a result, I had two offers within ten weeks and selected the one that scored highest. It has been the best match for my needs for my entire career.

WHAT IS THE RISK OF IGNORING YOUR IDEAL JOB PROFILE?

As I mentioned at the beginning of the book, focus is essential for an efficient and effective job search. By developing an IJP, you create a target for which you can then build communication and action plans to achieve your targeted role. If you develop a target and then ignore it or fail to develop a target in the first place, then your probability of landing a role that is an ideal match for your current needs is near zero. Effectively, you are relying on dumb luck. I do not know if you are that dumb, but I strongly doubt you are that lucky. Unfortunately, this happens more often than you may realize.

Look at LinkedIn for positions in your field of interest. Look at the duration of their job stints at senior levels. For many folks, you will see a series of one-to-two-year stints. For a minority of leaders, you will see multiple extended stays, potentially with one or more promotions. The reality is that those who select their next role with careful thought are more likely to weather executive suite changes and challenging economic times.

The danger of ignoring your IJP is real. I have seen too many leaders severely damage their ability to land an ideal role because they either try to skip or ignore their IJP during their pursuit. Tragically, people who have a strong work history for an extended time are very uncomfortable being in a career transition. As a result, they may lunge at the first opportunity that comes up. If they are a poor fit and they do not get the role, they risk looking desperate to the people in the search, thus undermining their reputation. If they do secure a job that is not an ideal fit, they and the company that hired the wrong person will soon discover it, resulting in a very short stay. This is very damaging to one's ability to land the next role because one would need to be able to successfully explain that although they were wrong to pursue the last role, their clarity and judgment has improved such that they can convince them that the new role is an ideal fit. In a competitive environment, who wants that extra baggage?

TOOL B: THE MARKETING DOCUMENT

The Marketing Document is second in importance and sequencing for a time-efficient and effective job search. The Marketing Document, or "MD" for short, is your primary tool when conducting networking meetings. Why not use the resume? The resume is historical in nature, whereas the Marketing Document is future-oriented. I cannot help you with where you have been, but I can help you get to where you want to go.

The resume review process is an exercise in "negative filtering." Reviewers are looking for a reason to eliminate a candidate from advancing in the interview process. Since the resume is supposed to be a summary of your work history and qualifications, it will provide the data for others to draw conclusions rightly or wrongly about you. For example, here are possible arguments that could be made against you:

- you have too little experience in the industry or role you are targeting

- your employment gaps and or short tenures indicate an issue with your work style
- you have worked too long in your last role, so you may not be open to change
- you are too old or too young for the role
- your education is not impressive
- your former employers and/or job titles are not impressive
- it is not clear how the role you are seeking is a natural extension of the recent roles you have had previously

The Marketing Document is a concise and focused framework to communicate your IJP, your value proposition to perform in that role, as well as identify the companies that will most likely have the role and environment you seek.

Visit **JohnPatrickHughes.com/templates**
for your free download of all templates.

COMPONENTS

Contact Information—The first component of your MD is your contact information, which should be brief. Just put your name and how to reach you, by phone number, email, or both. Don't use pronouns, age, or even specifics about where you're from, as all these things could get you "screened out" of the process.

Targeted Role(s)—Ideally, you'll have one or a maximum of two roles to list on your MD. They should be similar in both company size and functionality. If the roles are too dissimilar, then your MD becomes confusing, and it is clear you have not accurately defined your IJP or you have lost consistency in your messaging. Be prepared to explain why each role is appropriate versus the other.

Areas of Expertise—At this point in your career, you'll have cultivated many important skills and have knowledge in many subjects. You'll need to tailor this section specifically to fit your targeted roles. Determine what is relevant to your IJP and keep it between eight and twelve areas. Sequence and group them by relevance so each column presents a set of skills that work together.

Companies of Interest—The final component is trifurcating your companies of interest into three separate groups. This allows people to better understand the roles you are targeting and provides further clarity so they have an easier time helping you. Being specific leads to progress here. Providing specific companies of interest helps convey to others where you best believe you fit in the industry. Think of it this way, if you told someone you were looking for a role with a multi-billion-dollar global consumer packaged goods company, they may or may not know what firms you seek to contact. However, if you tell them you are looking to connect with firms like The Coca-Cola˙

Company, Unilever˚, and Nestlé˚, they will precisely understand the specific type of firms you are targeting. They may have contacts at the particular firms you mentioned, or they may revert with offers to introduce you to their contacts at PepsiCo˚, Colgate-Palmolive˚, or Hershey's˚.

Group them based on company size or industry. For example, if your role would change based on the size of the company, the left column may be firms over X millions of dollars, the middle column might be companies under a certain amount of money, and the right column might be private equity firms or bankers because they're the ones who control the companies you're targeting. It might be that you were in a highly regulated industry, so one column might be telecommunications, the next one might be banking, and the third one might be utilities. Although the industries are different, they share the trait of being highly regulated, which is your strength. You want to help people think more broadly about your background yet target companies most likely to value your skills and experiences.

Once you figure out what your three columns will be, the hard part is to determine how to populate the various cells on this document. If you're staying close to your industry, you want to consider who your competitors in your last job were, what companies are selling into the same client set you had in your last job, or it might be a different product or service altogether. There are different business journals that publish lists of companies. Get a subscription to that journal and then have access to their listing of companies. There are online services you can subscribe to, but they can be expensive, so you'll want to pool that expense with a collection of friends who are also in transition. One that comes to mind that I've used repeatedly is ZoomInfo' (*www.zoominfo.com*).

Every company you put down on that page is like entering a lottery. So, if you've got forty-five companies on the page, you're effectively listing yourself in forty-five lotteries and giving yourself forty-five points of future connections when you meet with somebody. By being specific about your targeted companies, you make it easier for others to understand your goals and put them in a better position to make a connection for you.

When you put this list together, within each column, you need to have at least one blank space, and it should not be the same line for all three columns. The reason for this is that the mind abhors a vacuum, and when someone is looking at this document for the first time and they see a blank space, in their mind they see an incomplete document and feel compelled to fill in that space. It increases the level of engagement with people you meet. Through editing and adding suggestions, they become more engaged with your search and gain a better understanding of your goals, which hopefully will produce more fruitful results.

HOW TO USE YOUR MARKETING DOCUMENT

The MD is primarily used when conducting one-on-one networking meetings. It is a framework for a structured conversation, helping you maintain a "future focus" and hopefully progress against the roles you are targeting.

The first step is to walk through the document with the person you are meeting and briefly explain your value proposition, targeted roles, and the areas of expertise you have developed that enable you to deliver for the roles you are targeting. You then need to check for confirmation that they completely understand what you have shared with them. Although you have a deep and nuanced understanding of your value proposition and the basis for it, everyone has their own lingo and frame of reference. That is why you need to have the conversation to confirm they understand and accept the validity of your value proposition. This is a good time to selectively share some of your work experiences and accomplishments. It is not intended to be a complete rehash of your career and resume, just enough to convince them you can deliver the value proposition you espouse.

The next step is to move on to the Companies of Interest section and explain how your value proposition can be applied to each of the trifurcated columns/categories/industries. You then explain your rationale for selecting the companies. This could include information about the companies or their leaders you have gleaned from research and other networking meetings or you may have worked for one of their competitors in the past or you have experience with the same suppliers or customers. You can then mention that your list is incomplete, and you are looking for their suggestions on companies to add or delete. The compatibility of their suggestions to your IJP and targeted companies will be a strong indicator of their degree of understanding and alignment with your objectives. If they suggest companies that are (to you) a clear mismatch to your targets, it indicates this is the right time to re-explain what you are targeting and why.

If a person is willing to meet you for a networking meeting, they are likely to want to help you. As you discuss your Companies of Interest, probe for opportunities for introductions and recording their insights. However, you cannot afford to go down a rabbit hole by following up an introduction to a person at a company that is clearly not a match for your IJP. If you do so, the person you are referred to will quickly identify the mismatch as well, and it will damage the relationship between the original referrer, mismatched referee, and you. To avoid this costly mistake, you can use the MD to explain that although you appreciate the offer of an introduction, the company they are connected to is not a good match for your targeted roles and you would rather wait for an introduction to one of your targets at a later date.

When you are about two-thirds through your meeting time, take a pause from the discussion of target companies and ask them how you can help them. As someone running around meeting people and attending events, you are likely aware of networking events, association meetings, and news articles of potential interest to them. By doing so, you demonstrate that you are interested in a reciprocal relationship of assistance and looking for opportunities to stay connected.

The close of the meeting has three elements:

1. Ensure a shared understanding of your value proposition and the types of roles and companies you are seeking.

2. Confirm the people and companies with whom they will make an introduction for you. I encourage you to offer to send them a draft of the introduction. This has two benefits. It makes it easier for them to make the introduction, which increases the probability it will occur. Secondly, it allows you to strongly influence the messaging, which should increase the probability the receiver will respond positively.

3. Ask them at what time intervals they would like to receive an update on your progress.

The post-meeting follow-up is as important as the meeting itself. Remember, it is not about activity, it is about progress! Assuming you met the person before work, <u>by noon that day,</u> you must send the person:

- a thank you note for their time and consideration
- your MD now updated to reflect the additions and subtractions of Companies of Interest discussed in your meeting
- a meeting recap of the introduction(s) they promised to make
- a draft of the introduction for them to edit and send on your behalf
- a request that they copy you on the introduction so you can follow up directly to set up a meeting with the referral target

If during your discussion, you identified networking events, association meetings, and news articles of potential interest to them, then do <u>not</u> send that information at this time. However, you should reference in your note that you're gathering the information and will revert in a couple of days with it. After three days, if you have not been copied on an introduction note, send the promised information of interest to the original person, thank them again for the offer of an introduction, and remind them to copy you when sending it.

If no response or introduction is received after another three days, send another note and ask them if they need any additional information to make the introduction. At this point, understand there is real resistance to making the introduction. It could be as benign as the person is just too busy with other pressing priorities. More likely, it is due to either the person not having a strong enough connection with the target to provide an introduction that will be well received, or the person is not confident your profile will be viewed as bringing value to the receiving party. Either way, it is better to drop the follow-up for this specific introduction and stay connected to the original person via a regular cadence of reconnecting emails with your ever-changing list of Companies of Interest within your MD.

TOOL C: IN-TRANSITION BUSINESS CARD

While your Marketing Document is your primary tool when conducting in-person networking, your in-transition business card is the companion piece for your meetings. Some folks may object that this is a remnant of the "Boomer" culture. It is not. When looking for your next role, it does not matter how many people you know, what matters is how many people think of you when the right role becomes available.

Many corporations have ceased issuing business cards, somewhat counterintuitively, but I believe the business card has become more impactful than in the past. They might even make a note on the card regarding your conversation they felt was relevant. The in-transition business card is another layer in the reinforcement of your messaging by concisely communicating your value proposition, your core skills, the role you are seeking, and how to best contact you.

During an in-person meeting, provide the other person with your card and ask for theirs. Assuming they do not have one, ask them to use the contact information on your card to email their contact information to you. Likely, they will add your card to the stack on their desk. Naturally, you will connect on LinkedIn and be one of the thousand or more LinkedIn contacts for which they have little to no recollection of where and why you are connected. However, when they do encounter a job opportunity or networking contact, they can scan the relatively small pile of cards on their desk to find yours with your value proposition and career targets.

As mentioned at the beginning of the book, consistent messaging is a central theme. The content of the business card reflects it and is copied from your MD. On the front of the card are the three methods of contact: email address, cell number, and LinkedIn ID. It should also have your abbreviated value proposition and the job title(s) you are seeking. The back of the card should contain a truncated list of your primary areas of expertise.

A final point to make is to use the heaviest paper stock available. You are an executive looking for your next leadership role. Spend a few extra dollars to have a business card that reflects your quality.

Visit Visit **JohnPatrickHughes.com/templates**
for your free download of all templates.

TOOL D: THE POWER GROUP AND THE POWER GROUP ACTIVITY REPORT (PGAR)

The Power Group is your personal board of directors for your professional career. They are an essential source of insightful coaching, feedback, and a force multiplier for your networking connections. A Power Group is composed of four to six peers. This size has proven optimal to ensure there are enough attendees to draw their support, but not so large that meetings become too unwieldy to address the needs of each member sufficiently. The more successful groups are based on a "pay it forward" attitude. If each of the members focuses on the needs of the others, then each member will have all the support they need from the group.

When forming the group, it is best to look for members who share a defining professional connection. The connection could be based on functional expertise or industry. Examples of functional grouping include sales and marketing, finance and accounting, and operations and logistics. Examples of industries where industry experience is a barrier to entry include healthcare, oil and gas, and private equity.

Each group can set up their own rules of operation. For example, a group I have been in since 2008 set up the following rules:

- *Decide on the weekly cadence of meetings.* Originally, when all in the group were in career transition, we met in person mid-morning on Mondays. We selected this time slot to ensure that it wouldn't interfere with times normally used for meeting with working executives and also act as a springboard for a productive week of job searching. In time, as most members landed jobs and several moved to different cities, the meetings moved to a video call held on the weekend.
- *Consistent attendance is a requirement.* Acceptable absences are due to vacation, illness, or a "family situation." Repeated absences are cause for being removed from the group. This might seem harsh, but since the purpose of membership is to help the other members, one needs to participate consistently.
- *Proposed new members attend a meeting on a provisional basis.* The existing members then vote on whether to approve them as a permanent member. Again, this may seem harsh, but as this group acts as a

mutual advisory board for all involved, an environment of mutual trust is essential.

- ***One's participation in their Power Group should not end when they land their next job.*** As I previously stated, high performing Power Groups operate under the premise that if each member's focus is being a resource to the other members, then everyone will receive all the support and guidance they will need. Besides, there is a wealth of advice the group can provide to a working team member, such as:

- ***Coaching on technical issues at work***—At one time, I had a consulting assignment of conducting a business valuation in Latin America. Several members of my group had done valuations in the United States and were able to provide detailed advice that proved quite helpful.

- ***Feedback and insight*** on how to best handle organizational and personnel dynamics and challenges in your new organization. The group members will have considerable experience in dealing with similar issues from which they can share "lessons learned."

- ***Opportunities*** to share your expanding network of contacts with your Power Group.

- ***The regular reminders of the challenges*** your peers and friends are facing while trying to secure their next executive role will provide you with perspective on how fortunate you are to be in your current role, which in turn will enable you to be more clear-headed about the challenges and frustrations within your current position.

- ***Be able to share your successes*** with folks who can truly appreciate the challenges you overcame.
- ***All jobs at the executive level are temporary.*** The group will help you detect the warning signs and assist you in ramping up your job search before it is too late.

My Power Group has been meeting weekly since 2008. Meetings are generally happy, constructive discussions, none happier than when the last person lands the role they were seeking. However, by the next week, the reality dawns on us all that it is not natural for all of us to be fully employed simultaneously, so we actively seek to determine who is at risk of losing their role and start working on a defense strategy and a job search plan.

It is important to note that the Power Group is not intended to replace participating in networking groups and events. They are complementary to each other and serve different purposes. We will discuss networking groups later in the book.

The Power Group Activity Report (PGAR) is the discussion framework for the Power Group meetings. Personally, I have been in too many networking meetings that devolve into a gripe session about the job market or drift into a variety of tangential "conversational cul-de-sacs." Its use ensures a time-efficient and effective format to maintain a focus on progress rather than activity.

Visit **JohnPatrickHughes.com/templates**
for your free download of all templates.

During each meeting, each member in turn uses the framework to address the four sections to the PGAR:

Section One: Current Events/Synopsis—Briefly and concisely share with the group the current state of the various opportunities they are currently pursuing. As part of this discussion, they will detail how each of these opportunities "scores" against their IJP. The group is responsible for conducting a Q&A to provide coaching and feedback on the individual pursuits and, when appropriate, challenge the member on whether a given opportunity scores well enough against the IJP to be worth further pursuit. When in a career transition, there is a natural inclination to use a liberal interpretation of what constitutes a valid job to chase. However, time is at a premium, so one should remain true to their IJP and leverage the feedback from their Power Group to maintain focus on progressing toward an ideal next role.

Section Two: Progress Against "Action Steps" Identified in the Prior Meeting—During the prior meeting, you will have self-identified or been assigned by the group specific action steps to advance your job search. The action steps could entail a range of activities, including contacting companies regarding the next step in the interview process, abandoning pursuits of roles that score too low against your IJP, attending networking groups, joining professional associations, following up with a networking introduction offered by a group member, updating one's resume/marketing document/LinkedIn profile, and action steps that seem relevant. At this juncture, it is essential for the members to enforce accountability on each other to stay on the path of progress.

Here is a personal example. At one time, I was trying to set up a fractional consulting practice. Setting up an LLC is a requisite to protect one's assets from litigation arising from the consulting practice. I promised the group I would have the LLC in place by the next meeting. When I did not keep my promise, at the next meeting, they excoriated me for not following through and leaving me financially exposed. Rightfully, I had the LLC in place by the following meeting.

Section Three: Assistance Needed from the Power Group Members—As progress is a central tenant in this process, always be prepared to share at least three specific networking connections or acts of assistance needed. Given that your Power Group members have a deep understanding of your IJP and value proposition, this is an ideal time to make forward progress in your job search. Surprisingly, many people are not well prepared for this section.

Examples of requests for assistance:

- Ask for honest feedback on whether your IJP is best classified as delusional for the current geographic and economic conditions, or ask them to "sanity-check" the scoring of your open opportunities against your IJP.
- Request coaching on how to best negotiate the terms of a job offer or on how to best approach or phrase your follow-up activity for your open pursuits.
- Ask for an introduction to a specific person or company from the targeted list on your MD, insight, and feedback on networking groups or business associations, or recommendations on resume or LinkedIn consultants.
- You could also ask for feedback on physical appearance, dress style, and/or emotional projection (are you coming across as panicked/desperate/angry/depressed?).

Section Four: Action Steps to Take by the Next Meeting—As we talked about at the beginning of the book, progress rather than activity is a central, underlying theme. What is the sense of being in a Power Group and participating in a PGAR meeting unless you are then taking the best steps to move your search forward to your ideal job? The action steps identified in this section then become your "homework" for your next PGAR.

Your "homework" may be identified by yourself, recommended by other group members, or something assigned to another member that you recognize as a valuable next step for your own search. The specific activities will arise from the discussion of the first three sections.

It could be coaching on how to best follow up on your open pursuits or to "score" your open pursuits against your IJP to better prioritize the pursuits you should continue and, just as importantly, which ones to drop so you can maintain focus on availability for the best options for you. It could be instruction from the group that you need to do a more thorough job on an action step from section two. It could be following up on the offer of networking assistance by contacting person "A" for an introduction to person "B."

A final thought on the Power Group and the PGAR is executive roles are a "merry-go-round" where each of us will get on and off several (too many?) times in our career, and we never know when the music will stop for us. An effective Power Group is an ideal vehicle to vent, laugh, learn, know that others have your back, and maintain forward progress on one's search for the ideal job.

TOOL E: STAIRCASE TO SUCCESS TRACKING DOCUMENT

This template is a tracker used to monitor and measure progress in your job search. It is based on several underlying principles.

What gets measured gets managed. To maintain a focus on progress vs. activity, one sets a weekly goal for a variety of job search elements and measures against those goals.

There is a hierarchy of activities to a job search. Normally, one starts their job search with lower-level activities, which then leads to the mid-level steps that, in turn, open the door to the higher-level activities, which ultimately provide access to a job offer.

Course corrections are key. Try to avoid the insanity of making the same mistake week after week. Time is precious when you do not have an income. Each week, it is essential to record what worked and what did not. If you received positive feedback about your job search approach in a given week, ensure you repeat it in the following weeks. By the same token, if something is not working, make a course correction the following week.

Create the world you want to live in by sharing job leads. You cannot control when you will find your ideal job, but you can contribute to the volume of job opportunities within your network. You may think you are the perfect fit for a given job opportunity, but the reality is that the true job description is unspoken and resides in the back of the hiring executive's head. By sharing job leads, you reconnect with others in a very positive way and remind them of the role you seek.

An explanation of the progression of "steps" and the goals for each:

Applying Via Internet Postings—The weekly goal is <u>zero.</u> One should review the Internet daily for job postings of interest but only do so before 7:00 a.m., as it is too early to interact with people. You should not be searching websites during the workday. That time is for meeting and contacting people. It is best to set up job search alerts based on the characteristics of your ideal job, on the relevant search engines, and on specific companies you are targeting or have listed on your MD. However, do not load your resume to these sites. If you do so, you lose control of it and enable companies to make decisions in a vacuum based on how they perceive your relative fit for a role.

Most companies that post jobs online use filtering software to review resumes, greatly reducing the number of resumes they physically need to review. This filtering algorithm is your enemy. At this point in your career, it is highly likely it will screen you out due to a myriad of reasons: too old, career gaps, too long in a job, too short in a job, prior job titles, the prevalence of "buzz words" they are filtering to identify a desired candidate, and others we cannot imagine.

The goal of reviewing the Internet postings is to identify roles that are a solid match to your IJP and then network with the key people in that targeted company to discuss the role and how your skills and experiences would enable you to be successful there. Although highly helpful, you need not network with the hiring executive. The key is to find a "sympathetic ear." They will likely ask you to apply online but reference their referral. In many companies, an internal referral from an executive will cause your application to skip the automated filtering process and be reviewed by a person. To enhance your probability of securing an initial screening interview, ask your internal contact to reach out to the hiring executive and/or HR department to ask for your qualifications to be considered.

Recruiter Interactions—The weekly goal depends on the recruiters in your network. The term "recruiter interactions" should be considered broadly. It can range from an in-person meeting to a three-minute conversation at a networking event, to a phone call, to an email, or just a quick text exchange. The weekly targeted recruiter interactions will depend upon the number of recruiters in your network and the frequency and manner in which they want you to reconnect with them. If you do not know, then ask them. The content of the reconnect should be putting a positive light on your job search process and reminding them what type of role you seek.

Meetings with Both Industry/Executive Associations and In-Transition Groups—The weekly goal is three events due to a variety of reasons. First, attending events is an investment of significant time in preparation, travel, attendance, and follow-up. Second, there is also the financial cost of the events or membership as well as transportation costs, which are not insignificant, especially when you are unemployed. Finally, there is a limit to the number of available group meetings every week that are relevant to your IJP.

Networking meetings tend to fall into two basic categories. Ones primarily attended by working professionals and ones where the attendees are in career transition. Neither category is more important to your search. Each serves a slightly different purpose. At events attended by working professionals, you may be able to meet with people who work for the companies you are targeting or who are at least in peer positions to your targets and can assist you in networking with them. In addition, working executives are often contacted by retained recruiters regarding open positions, so they can help you network with those recruiters and potentially those open positions.

Events for people in career transition provide an opportunity to meet with many people eager to make new connections, so you will be able to expand your network and greatly improve your ability to network with target companies. Regardless of the type of event, the goals of attending are to identify several people you want to have an individual follow-up discussion with and set the commitment/date with them at the event.

One-on-One Meetings with Both Working Executives and In-Transition People—The weekly goal is five events, and here is why. First, this is the most effective activity you can engage in to generate progress toward your ideal job. There are also only a total of ten breakfast or lunchtime slots in a week, so booking half of them provides enough time for timely follow-ups and flexibility to reschedule meetings when necessary. These meetings are also heavy consumers of time and expense, so you need to be judicious that each meeting provides a good probability of progressing your job search toward your ideal job.

Like networking group meetings, one-on-one meetings fall into two basic categories: meeting with working professionals and meeting with a person in career transition. Again, neither category is more important than the other because each serves a slightly different purpose. Working executives will have deep knowledge of their current firm and, to a lesser degree, about their former firm. These meetings are most productive when the person works in one of the companies you are targeting. The goals in these conversations include helping them understand your value proposition and IJP such that they are comfortable enough to:

- be your advocate
- initiate an introduction(s) to other business leaders within their company
- initiate an introduction(s) to leaders within other firms on your MD

Meeting with people in a career transition can be valuable as well. In-transition professionals will have shallow knowledge of quite a few companies, as well as deep knowledge of networking groups and trends in the job search process. These meetings are most productive when you are just starting your job search but are still valuable throughout. The goals in these conversations are the same as the ones you have when speaking with a working professional.

Regardless of the employment status of the person you are meeting, the goal is to be focused on an introduction that brings you closer to your ideal role. Some career coaches stress getting three incremental introductions from each meeting. I firmly believe that quality over quantity leads to progress. As long as the person you are meeting understands your value proposition and the ideal job you seek to the extent that they would be an advocate for you, then you have had a productive meeting. You just need to have the patience and faith that you can activate that connection when they are in a position to make an introduction that actually drives your job search forward.

Interviews (Screening or with a Hiring Executive)—The weekly goal is one. We would all like to have a half dozen interviews per week, but that is not a reasonable expectation for a focused job search at the executive level.

There is no value in getting caught up in the semantics of whether it is a screening interview or an interview with a hiring executive. The important thing to focus on is that the one-on-one meetings and leveraging of your network regarding Internet job postings result in at least one interview per week. Progressing through multiple interview layers for a single job still counts toward your total.

Now that we have discussed the progression of steps let's look at how to use the Tracking Document. Once a week, record your activity by "step" and calculate your variance (plus or minus) to the goal. Reflect upon your successes and challenges during the week and repeat the behaviors or make the course corrections necessary to position yourself for a better result the next week. At the beginning of your search, your activity will be heavily weighted to the lower steps. In time, you should have a more dispersed distribution of activity. Over time, the Tracking Document will highlight where you have plateaued. At this point, examine your activity to identify what you are doing incorrectly. If you can't identify the issue, you may need to drill down to a lower step to see what caused you to get off track.

Once you have been consistently achieving one interview, five one-on-one meetings, and attending three association/networking meetings per week, congratulate yourself for having a productive and efficient job search. The scoring confirms that you have been working effectively, so you just need to have a bit more patience and faith that the "career merry-go-round" will soon invite you for another ride. During my extended searches, when I have been achieving my Staircase to Success goals by Thursday evening, I have taken Friday off from my job search (without guilt) and used the time to refresh and recharge by catching a movie matinee, hitting golf balls at the driving range, or binge-watching TV.

Visit **JohnPatrickHughes.com/templates**
for your free download of all templates.

THE FIVE TOOLS SUMMARY

A job search system and a weight loss program are similar in that they have several components that are best used together for maximum results. However, many folks tend to embrace the elements to varying degrees, and as a result, they suboptimize the impact. For instance, losing weight is a function of exercise, dieting, sleep, and stress management. Engage in all the elements in the right measure, you will see results. However, if you limit your engagement to only a few of the elements, you will be frustrated by the limited progress and will abandon the program. These five tools are quite similar. Each of them will assist you in your job search, but they are most effective when utilized together.

The IJP is the cornerstone of your search. It informs your MD sections for your value proposition, targeted role(s), and companies of interest. The value proposition from your MD is "cut and pasted" into your resume and LinkedIn profile and is condensed into a few words onto your business card. The areas of expertise from your MD are on the back of your business card. The Power Group and PGAR provide regular accountability checkpoints and informed resources for feedback on your job search process to ensure you are making timely course corrections on your job search and to sanity-check that your IJP is not delusional. The Staircase for Success tracking document provides an objective visual picture of your progress and highlights at what "step" you have plateaued so you can engage the insight of your Power Group for guidance.

CHAPTER 6

NETWORKING

NETWORKING VS. JOB SEARCHING

All too often, people mistakenly conflate networking and job searching. Although they share certain elements, they are different activities. It is important to understand the difference to ensure long-term success.

Networking is a continual process of originating and then maintaining relationships with a wide range of people to establish your personal and professional brands. Like a shiny coat of varnish, it becomes impervious by applying many "thin layers of interactions" that consistently demonstrate behavior that reinforces your personal and professional brands. As a result, you cannot burst onto the scene and claim to have a brand of "X." Your personal and professional brands are not what you say they are. They are what you consistently demonstrate by your actions and what the market perceives of them.

Hopefully, it helps to share an example of the two brands. My personal brand is that I try to help everyone I meet to achieve their personal and professional objectives, whether it is providing advice and counsel, connecting them to another friend or contact within my network, or introducing them to the correct service leader within my firm. I am particularly known for effectively coaching executives in career transition and being a clearing house for talented people and great job opportunities. My professional brand is a highly organized account management/ business development leader who never sells but seeks to solve client problems with a level of client care that is unmatched. As you can see, one cannot claim these brands. One needs to demonstrate them by consistently modeling these behaviors and building relationships with peers through many sincere interactions in which they are not asking for a favor.

Please note, when discussing personal and professional branding, I am not talking about the gimmicky labeling you will see advocated in books focused on branding. I am talking about the authentic "you." People can detect a phony and resent being manipulated, so you risk significant damage to your reputation and marketability when you lack sincerity. To use a baseball analogy, if you claim you are a dominant hitter and can hit all kinds of pitches but, in reality, can only hit fastballs, you will be in trouble because baseball, like life in general, is filled with curveballs.

Job searching is a range of activities conducted for the time necessary to locate and land one's next role. Ideally, one will leverage their network of contacts when conducting the search so they can benefit from their established brands, giving them market acceptance. Assuming you have built up goodwill with your personal brand, people in your network will be predisposed to helping you in your job search by opening their network to you to pursue roles that align with the professional brand that you have consistently demonstrated to them.

As you can see, having a vibrant network provides for a "running head start" when beginning a job search. Unfortunately, too many people do not effectively invest or engage in a continuous networking effort. Many will claim that they are too busy at work. Given that all executive jobs are temporary, that is a truly stupid reason for failure. In over twenty years of helping executives find their next job, I have never met anyone who said they started networking too soon.

If you have not established a network previously, your job search will be more challenging as you will need to first build trust and brand awareness, and your behaviors initially will necessarily be one-sided. You are looking for assistance from strangers. Regardless, you must move forward with your job search. Let's look at the sequence of activities.

ASSESSING YOUR NETWORK

The first step in networking is to assess your network according to several dimensions. The first is their level of interest and commitment to aiding in your job search. Ones scoring highly in this area are people you may want to preview your IJP for feedback and schedule an extended discussion of your MD, during which you press for direct and potential indirect introductions to key people at your target companies, as well as feedback on your target company list. These are the folks you want to become vested in your search and keeping them in the loop for the duration will be an invaluable source of coaching, feedback, introductions, and job leads. In my experience, most job offers were originally sourced from first- or second-level introductions from the candidate's original network.

Another grouping paradigm is based on how you trifurcated your target companies on your MD. For example, if your targets are grouped by industry or the role evolves based on the size of the company, or your targets include private equity funds as well as corporations, you may need to tailor your approach and messaging.

An important stratification is categorizing your contacts as "A, B, or C players." It may sound judgmental; it is, and it is necessary. Whether it is on sports teams, study groups in school, or co-workers, we are well aware of the existence of A, B, and C players. It is essential that you make this assessment so you can identify which group is your "lane" for networking. One group is not necessarily better than the other. The key is to be in the lane that is a natural fit for you, so you can be most effective in your networking and job search. At this point, you must be honest with yourself about which lane is yours. Mankind has a pack mentality, and we naturally seek to be in the right pack. As you talk with your peers, you will innately sense with whom you have a natural fit. The need for aligning yourself to your correct lane is clear.

If you are a B player and are networking with other B players, they will appreciate and value your career experiences and challenges and will feel comfortable making introductions to other B players. B players are contacted regarding B-level job opportunities, for which you may be competitive. If a B player tries networking with A players, their career experiences and challenges are likely not to be properly appreciated and valued and they may be reluctant to make introductions to their A player contacts. Similarly, if a B player tries to network with C players, their skills and experiences may appear overpowering and threatening, which causes them to be reluctant to make introductions.

If you are unsure what lane a given person resides in, use their job history on LinkedIn as an imperfect guide.

A players' work history will show steady progression to senior roles with significant accomplishments. Their tenure may be two to three years as they were hired to fix a particular problem and then moved on to the next challenge.

B players' work history may show them at the senior or one level down with middling accomplishments. Their tenure may be extended as they demonstrate consistent performance.

C players' work history may show them at the senior or one level down with middling accomplishments. Their tenure will likely be one to two years due to the inherent struggles of C-level companies and their incomplete skill set. By the way, C players are often the best at networking and job searching as they understand the importance of maintaining a vibrant network for their own job search needs.

I want to reiterate that one lane is not better than the other. There are A-, B-, and C-level companies and job opportunities. The key is to know your lane and stick to it so you can efficiently and effectively progress your job search.

You cannot control the frequency of assistance you receive during your networking and job searching, but you can control how much you help others. Everyone needs help, so I suggest you share as many job leads as possible (whether you are working or in career transition), and be generous with your time with others seeking assistance in their networking and job search and do it without the expectation of immediate reciprocity. Helping someone in need of assistance is a great way to stay on the "radar screen" of others, and it is the right thing to do. People who have a positive and helpful approach tend to attract other like-minded people, so have faith that they will help you when you need it.

GETTING THE MOST OUT OF NETWORKING EVENTS

The process of networking is a continuous cycle of attending professional association and networking group events, identifying people worthy of an in-depth conversation, and then conducting a one-on-one meeting with the targeted people. Let's look at these two essential activities in turn.

Preparation

As progress rather than activity is a central theme of this program, preparation is essential to making this a productive and efficient use of time and money. If you are attending a group meeting for the first time, you will want to be escorted by a friend who is a member or reach out to the chapter leader and ask them if you can attend as their guest so you can learn more about the group and consider becoming a member. Anyone who puts in the volunteer work to lead a group would feel validated by the interest of others to potentially join the group. As an added benefit, if you are attending as a guest of the leader, there is often no charge.

Once you register for the meeting, reach out to the administrator (by phone if possible) for the group and ask if there is a registration list they can share. Normally, this list would not be shared with outsiders, but if you let them know you want to do some prior research before the meeting, they may share some information. The important thing is that you have connected with the most knowledgeable person in the group who knows everybody.

If you are an existing member of the group, you should be able to receive an event registration list a few days prior. Even if it is not a final listing, it will provide plenty of useful data. Print out whatever list you have. Take the data and cross-check it against LinkedIn to identify people who are currently working (or in their prior role) at one of your target companies. Make a note of an aspect of their work history that could be woven into your initial conversation with them.

You need to know the dress code for the specific event. Ask the person who is escorting you, the chapter leader, or the group administrator. Ensure you are dressing at the same level of formality as the majority of the members or slightly more formal. Show respect for the group and its membership. That means your clothes are neatly pressed (no jeans) and your shoes are shined. You may mistakenly think that this is a minor detail, but it is not. You will be surrounded by people who do not know you, so the first message they receive from you is the care you take in your physical appearance.

A final step of preparation is to do some cursory research on the speaker and the topic. You may think this is a lot of work, and you are right. So, do not short-change yourself by skipping steps. There is a reason your goal is only three events per week. It takes a sizable investment in time to make an event a highly productive activity.

Working the Room

To effectively "work the room," your actions should be broken down into phases.

Arrive thirty minutes before the registration table is opened. At this time, the administrator will be setting up the nametags. This is an ideal opportunity to acknowledge whatever assistance they provided to you prior to the event, review the nametags of those who are registered (which may contain their company name), and ask for their advice on who to meet at the event. Ask them to introduce you to some of your targeted people. I suggest you hang around the registration table and introduce yourself as a prospective new member to the other early arrivals, with a particular focus on the people you are targeting.

The speaker will arrive several minutes before the event start time. Normally, they are trying to get a vibe for the group and sometimes they are a bit nervous. This is an ideal time to approach the speaker and ask them a couple of questions on their topic based on your prior research. Undoubtedly, this will make a favorable impression when they are ready and willing to absorb your conversation. Then, exchange business cards, advise that you will be sending a LinkedIn connection request, and confirm follow-up activity (if any).

If you are in a career transition, do not mention it during your discussion. Mention it during a future discussion. Keep the focus on them as a professional and the subject matter of their presentation. You would be surprised by how many people attend an event and approach the speaker without any knowledge or forethought on the topic at hand. It is important to note it is a waste of time to initiate a conversation with the speaker after their presentation. At that time, their energy levels have dropped, and they are being bombarded by a long stream of people trying to make their introductions, asking the same questions, and saying the same things. All those people are likely to blur together for the speaker. As the speaker is starting to head out the door, swing back to them, thank them for their presentation and remind them of the follow-up action you will be taking.

As the crowd starts to build, move over to the central point where the members are congregating, which is often the bar or food table. Do not eat or drink. You are there to make connections. Keep your hands free to shake hands and make notes on your list of registrants. It will be helpful to be visually interesting without being weird or promoting a point of view others may find objectionable. The goal is to provide potential conversation starters, not side-track a potential interaction with some aspect of your personal life.

Examples of conversation starters include:

- Jewelry that sparkles or other eye-catchers, such as stylish scarves, ties, and pocket squares, usually start a conversation
- Lapel pins with a company logo, U.S. flag, or lapel pins with a benign personal interest will also work. I wear a shamrock pin my nephew gave me. He works in the Irish Consulate, and I went to grad school in Dublin, so it leads to an easy conversation
- A colorful cocktail begs people to guess what they are. I favor a Mai Tai—fun for conversation and fun to drink
- Visible injuries such as a foot cast, arm sling, or eye patch always draw attention. One of the most successful networking events I ever attended was when the dress code was suit and tie, and I had one foot in one of those clunky compression boots. To avoid aggravating my

foot, I stood next to a table so my foot was protected by it. I had a steady stream of people walking up to me to hear about the injury, and they were naturally predisposed to helping me, as my presence at the event demonstrated that I do not let challenges slow me down

Examples of things not to wear include:

- Lapel pins of a political or social issue or nature are best avoided. For every person who may agree with you, there is likely one who does not. Why filter out half of the audience by asking them to first agree with a personal point of view instead of focusing on you as a professional?

- Religious symbols, depending on the event and part of the country, can fall into either the do or do not show category. It is totally understandable that religion is part of one's identity and something you can share at a one-on-one meeting if you sense the other person is receptive to it. However, when you are at a professional event trying to initiate relationships with strangers, don't force people to first decide how they feel about your religious affiliation. Keep the focus on your skills as a professional. Wear your symbols, but not overtly visible. If you live in a community where religious affiliation is important, then wear them proudly. This recommendation is made purely to increase your odds of success.

During the speaker portion of the event, sit at a table or row surrounded by people you haven't yet met. This will provide an opportunity to meet additional people during this portion of the event. More importantly, use this time to annotate your registration sheet with the follow-up activities you discussed with the various people you met so far at the event. Assuming one of the follow-ups was to send them a LinkedIn connection request, send it during the speaker portion.

When scripting the connection request note, mention that you will follow up tomorrow (or whenever agreed upon) on the other follow-up activities you discussed. People are bored easily and often will respond to the ping of a connection request from someone they met within the last thirty minutes. Now that you have a first level connection to them, search their connections for your target companies when you start your research the next day.

After the event, a queue will form around the speaker as various members want to introduce themselves. As you already talked to the speaker before the event, your focus is on the members waiting semi-patiently in line. Scan the name tags to identify a couple of folks you want to meet. You then approach them on the line at a ninety-degree angle with your back to the speaker (this indicates you are not trying to "cut in line." As they have nothing else to do as they wait, they should be open to talking with you. This is a handy way to kill time until you can say your final goodbye to the speaker (as referenced in the "speaker" section of this chapter). During this wrap-up period, circle back to the chapter leader/your escort and the chapter administrator and thank them for the event and their assistance.

Setting the Hook

Conducting an effective introductory conversation at an event is the most challenging. It is a lot like fly fishing. It requires a deft touch while you consider many factors. The goal is to have enough of an introductory conversation that creates interest in you without disclosing too much information that depletes the rationale for a follow-up meeting. For this aspect of the meeting, you will need to develop an internal clock and a series of questions you want to ask others, as well as a limited amount of information about yourself you intend to disclose. Most meetings have an open networking portion before the speaker of thirty to sixty minutes. In my experience, three minutes is the maximum amount of time you should spend with someone for whom you are trying to "set the hook" for a follow-up one-on-one discussion. If you discern you are talking to someone with whom it would not be productive to have a follow-up discussion, cut the conversation shorter.

The math would indicate you would have ten to twenty conversations. In reality, you will have six to twelve as time is spent locating your preferred targets and waiting for them to complete their prior conversations. Depending upon your comfort level of breaking into an ongoing conversation with people you do not know, consider doing so. This enables you to speak to two people simultaneously, which increases the odds that at least one of them will be worth a follow-up. It is also easier to disengage from a group discussion. Regardless of whether you are talking to one or more people, keep the focus of the discussion on them, the speaker, and the speaker's topic. You must resist the urge to tell your life story, recite your "elevator pitch," or blather on about being "screwed out" of your last job.

Examples of icebreaker topics to start a conversation:

- *Information you gleaned from your research on the speaker or the speaker's topic*—Do not render an opinion (as you do not know their thoughts on the subject), but you can share the opinions expressed in articles you read.
- *Ask if their company has been impacted by the recent economy*—Similarly, ask about their expectations about the economic outlook in the coming months.
- *Ask how long they have been a member of the group*—Let them know you are a prospective member and would appreciate their insights about the group and who else they recommend you meet. They may be able to walk you over to that person at the event.
- If they ask about your employment status, tell them *you recently completed your role of X at Y company and that you are currently assessing what you want to do next.* This is a good topic to create a reason for a future discussion by telling them you have several ideas regarding your next career step and would appreciate hearing their perspective over a coffee.

Since you are on a "three-minute clock," finding a clean way to exit a conversation depends upon whether you want to have a follow-up one-on-one conversation. If you do want to have a follow-up conversation, here are a few examples of exit statements:

- *"I enjoyed our brief conversation but do not want to monopolize your time. I would like to complete our introductions over coffee one morning. I will reach out tomorrow with potential dates and will send a LinkedIn connection request."*
- *"I enjoyed our brief conversation. I saw one of my friends over there who I promised to meet here. I would like to complete our introductions over coffee one morning. I will reach out tomorrow with potential dates and send a LinkedIn connection request."*
- *"I enjoyed our brief conversation. Please excuse me as I would like to refresh my drink/get some food before the presentation starts. I would like to complete our introductions over coffee one morning. I will reach out tomorrow with potential dates and will send a LinkedIn connection request."*

If you do not want to have a follow-up conversation, the exit statements are the same except exclude the mention of setting up a follow-up over coffee.

Follow-Up

The key to turning activity into progress is a timely follow-up. If your initial meeting is at an event before work, send the promised follow-up by noon. If the event was lunchtime, then by the end of the day. If it was an after-work event, then the following morning before 8:00 a.m., preferably by 7:00 a.m. The follow-up email should be friendly, concise, and focused on setting up the next meeting. Although in-person is much preferred, a video call can be productive as well. Here's an example of an initial follow-up email:

> *"Dear X,*
>
> *I enjoyed our brief conversation last night at X. As we discussed, I am reaching out to set up a time to complete our introductions over coffee before work. At present I am available on the Xth, X^{th}, or the Xth. Please advise what day, time, and part of town works well for you or if I should circle back in "X" weeks. I appreciate your time and consideration, and I am looking forward to our discussion."*

The rationale for this message structure is as follows:

- *Remind* the person where you met.
- *Minimize* the iteration of emails by providing specific meeting options such that one response from the target will provide enough information to send a meeting notice.

- *Circling back is* an important aspect because it gives the person unrestricted options and precludes them from simply saying they are not available.

You are requesting "coffee before work" because there is always a time before work, and an offer of coffee implies a lesser commitment of both time and money. You may end up having breakfast, but if you request it, you may be rebuffed with the excuse that they do not eat breakfast. Hopefully, they will respond right away, but if not, give them a week to respond and set a reminder. At that time, send a follow-up request for a meeting. It is essential that whenever following up, your tone is one of understanding for the delay and not exerting pressure. I suggest never using the phrase "follow up." Instead, use "circling back" or "checking in" and mention that you understand they are very busy.

If in two weeks you have not received a response, send a similar message. If they do not respond after the second follow-up email, drop the pursuit and focus on people who do want to meet with you. At that point, ask yourself why you were unable to secure the meeting. Did you share too much information at the networking event? Did you come across as too desperate, pushy, or otherwise off-putting? Were you dressed appropriately for the original networking event? If you are unsure of the root cause, discuss it with your Power Group to see if they can provide insight so you can make a course correction for the next event.

GETTING THE MOST OUT OF ONE-ON-ONE NETWORKING MEETINGS

Now that you set up a one-on-one meeting with a new contact let's discuss the strategy and process to make it a productive use of time.

Preparation

Assuming you connected with the targeted person on LinkedIn after the initial interaction at the networking event, you will want to do some basic research. Make a note of their company and career history. Is there any commonality with your own? Cross-check the executives in the companies you are targeting in your MD against the person you are going to meet.

Meeting Choreography

When meeting in person, ensure you arrive at least five minutes early. Email or text the other person to let them know you have arrived early, where you are sitting, and what you are wearing. This may sound pedantic, but you do not want to start off the meeting with an awkward search for the right person. I once had a guy join my table, and we were five minutes into the coffee when we realized he was at the wrong table! We had a good laugh, and he went on to meet the correct person. Fortunately, I had arrived early, so it did not interfere with my targeted person who arrived on time.

After your initial introductions, briefly walk them through your career progression. If you identified any company or history overlap, this would be a good time to mention it. The next step is to hand them your MD and walk them through your value proposition, core skills, jobs targeted, and companies of interest. Take your time discussing the individual companies and ask them if they have a connection to any of them, any information on developments at your targets, and any suggestions on companies to add to your company list for which they have a contact.

When a contact offers to connect you to a company not on your list, review it against the criteria you used to develop your companies of interest list. You are then empowered to politely decline introductions to companies that are not likely to have a role that meets your IJP. If you do accept the misguided introduction, the significant mismatch will be apparent right away. The third-party will be chafed that they wasted time on you and will likely share their frustration with the intermediary, which in turn will damage your relationship with them. For you, it will be a waste of time and money, as well as forfeiting the opportunity to build on that relationship for future introductions that could be productive.

After about two-thirds through your allotted time, stop and ask them how you can help them. As a by-product of your job search efforts, you have developed a network of contacts in industry, relationships with service providers, and an awareness of myriad business associations and networking groups that may be of interest to them. You may even be able to bring your new contact as a guest to one of the groups. This is valuable information to the working professional you are meeting. Demonstrating an interest in a reciprocal relationship of assistance greatly improves the dynamic with your new contact and can be the basis of developing a long-term relationship.

Close the meeting with a recap of the action steps and timing both parties agreed to take to ensure you have a common understanding.

Ask Three Things

For any one-on-one meeting, always come prepared to ask for three specific networking connections. If you are fortunate enough to meet a stranger who is open to meeting you one-on-one, they are likely open to be of assistance to you. Therefore, ensure the meeting is productive and satisfying to both parties by focusing on the specific introductions that are most central to your success.

Follow-Up

The follow-up process for one-on-one meetings is much the same as the effort to set up the meeting in the first place. Timely follow-up is essential for converting the meeting into a productive activity. The lapse time to send a follow-up is the same. If your initial meeting was before work, send the follow-up note by noon. If the meeting was lunchtime, then by the end of the day. If it was after work hours, then the following morning before 8:00 a.m., preferably by 7:00 a.m.

The follow-up email should also be friendly, concise, and focused on the action steps discussed in your meeting. An example of an initial follow-up email:

"Dear X

Thank you for your time and consideration to meet with me today. I enjoyed our conversation and learning more about your career path and company. As we discussed, I have attached a link to the article on X, meeting information for the Y group, and already made the introduction to service provider Z by separate email. Please let me know if you have any questions. I appreciate your offer to make an introduction to person A at company B, and person C at company D.

To facilitate the introduction, I have enclosed a draft as a thought starter you can easily customize. If possible, if you copy me on the email, I can follow up directly with person B to set up a meeting.

'Hello person A,

I recently met person G, who is a Finance/ Marketing/Operations Leader currently focused on building relationships in your industry, as well as his/her knowledge of the key business leaders. He/She specifically mentioned your company to be of interest.

I enjoyed my conversation with him/her, and I think you will as well.

As your busy schedule allows, I suggest you two have a conversation.'

The rationale for this message structure:

- *acknowledges* their kindness
- *demonstrates* you will keep your promise of assistance
- *makes it easy* for them to make the introductions to people you discussed in your meeting
- *minimizes* the iteration of emails by enabling you to follow up directly with the referral target
- *puts subtle pressure* on the referral target to have a conversation with you by being included in the referral note

The follow-up process is very similar. If you were copied on the referral note, reach out the following day to the referral target and copy the intermediary. Within your follow-up note, include specific dates and times for a coffee meeting or video call. If in two weeks you have not received a response, send a similar message. If they do not respond after the second follow-up email, drop the pursuit and focus on people who do want to meet with you.

If the person you met has not made the introductions you discussed in your meeting or the referral target has not responded to your requests for a meeting, reflect on what is blocking your progress. If it is the former situation, then it likely is due to one of two reasons:

- the person you met does not have a strong enough relationship with the referral target to make an introduction that they will accept (there is nothing you can do about that barrier)
- the person you met is not convinced that the referral target would find value in meeting you

Again, you must ask yourself why you were unable to secure the meeting. Did you come across as too selfish, desperate, pushy, or otherwise off-putting? Were you dressed appropriately? If you are unsure of the root cause, discuss it with your Power Group to see if they can provide insight so you can make a course correction for the next networking event.

CHAPTER 7

RECRUITERS

Now that you know how to effectively network on your own, let's look on how to best incorporate recruiters into your job search plan. The purpose of this section is to highlight the differences in the four types of recruiters and how to best interact with them.

GLOBAL RETAINED RECRUITERS

Types of Roles—CXO roles in large public and privately-held companies, as well as positions that directly report into these roles. The compensation packages range from mid to high six-figures. These roles tend to be either at good companies in undesirable cities or at lousy companies in good cities.

Their Value Proposition to Companies—They tell their clients they find candidates who are not looking or would otherwise not be discovered by the company. They put prospective candidates through an exhaustive process of multi-stage interviews, background checks, and professional reference reviews. The process will take months, and they will assemble a primary group of four to five candidates, as well as a backup group in case the client declines all candidates in the first group.

Candidates They Seek—Since they offer to provide "hidden candidates," they tend to include only one in-transition candidate in a panel. They also tend to favor candidates who have deep experience in a given industry versus limited experience in a range of industries.

How to Originally Connect and Maintain a Relationship with Them—As is the case with all recruiter types, maintaining a well-scripted LinkedIn profile that compellingly highlights your value proposition will be essential for your success. In terms of initiating contact with a global retained recruiter, the best path is usually via an email introduction by someone who has either hired the recruiter or been placed into a role by them. Follow up the e-introduction within a day via email and include your resume, IJP, and request a fifteen-minute introductory call.

Do not be offended if they do not respond. Their focus is on finding job orders to fill. They will contact you if and when they have a role for which you are an ideal match. If you do have an introductory discussion, you will want to ask them at what interval you should reconnect. As the default, follow up monthly with a brief email with a positive tone that reiterates your appreciation for them keeping you in mind for appropriate opportunities. Attach your resume and IJP.

Finally, their connections to companies are often via the board of directors. These directors often live in cities other than the company headquarters. As a result, retained searches for roles in your market are often being conducted by recruiters in other cities, so use your connections in other cities for introductions to global retained recruiters as well.

REGIONAL / LOCAL RETAINED RECRUITERS

Types of Roles—CXO roles in small public and medium to large privately-held companies, as well as positions that directly report into these roles. The compensation packages range from low to mid-six-figures. These roles tend to be within a defined geography, as they tend to develop deep roots within their area.

Their Value Proposition to Companies—They tell their clients that they find local candidates who are not looking or would otherwise not be discovered by the company without the cost of relocation expenses. Like global firms, they put prospective candidates through an exhaustive process of multi-stage interviews, background checks, and professional reference reviews. The process may take a couple of months but is more streamlined than the global firms.

Candidates They Seek—They also tend to include only one in-transition candidate in a panel and favor local candidates with deep experience in the client's industry. However, in my experience, they seem less concerned than the global firms about candidates having divided their careers among multiple industries.

How to Originally Connect and Maintain a Relationship with Them—Similar to global firms, maintaining a well-scripted LinkedIn profile that compellingly highlights your value proposition will be essential for your success is a given. Since they have widespread and deep bonds in your geography of interest, developing some level of a personal connection with them is quite important. Ask your local network for recommendations and introductions to regional/local retained recruiters. Follow up the e-introduction within a day via email and include your resume, IJP, and a request for a fifteen-minute introductory call.

Given their focus on developing an extensive local network, they are likely to be more open to having an initial discussion. Regardless, do not be offended if they do not respond. Their focus is also on finding job orders to fill. They will reach out to you if and when they have a role for which you are an ideal match. The same guidelines apply regarding follow-up. If you do have an introductory discussion, ask them at what interval you should reconnect. As the default, follow up monthly with a brief email using a positive tone that reiterates that you appreciate them keeping you in mind for appropriate opportunities. Attach your resume and IJP.

CONTINGENT RECRUITERS

Types of Roles—Generally the roles they are trying to fill are one or two levels below the CXO level in small to medium privately-held companies. The compensation packages range from low to mid-six-figures. These roles tend to be within a defined geography, as they tend to develop deep roots within their area.

Their Value Proposition to Companies—They offer their clients speed and are only paid if the candidate is hired. When a firm is utilizing contingent search, they often contact more than one firm. This creates an environment where speed of response is essential. The process is much more streamlined than that of retained firms and will be handled in weeks rather than months.

Candidates They Seek—Although working business leaders are generally preferred, there is wider acceptance of in-transition candidates. The sense of urgency to fill the role tends to engender more flexibility in meeting job specifications, as well as more openness to candidates in transition than when using retained firms.

How to Originally Connect and Maintain a Relationship with Them—Working with contingent search firms requires a very different approach. One still needs to maintain a well-scripted LinkedIn profile that compellingly highlights your value proposition, this will be essential for your success and remains a constant requirement. However, the quality and integrity of contingent recruiters can vary widely. I have heard too many instances of contingent recruiters submitting resumes for open positions without the permission of the candidate, whether or not they have an agreement with the firm to submit resumes. This could be disastrous to one's job search.

If you subsequently try to network into a company for which this has happened, or you have been knowingly submitted by another recruiter for a role, the company may reject your candidacy to avoid the commission claim from the first recruiter's submission of your resume. More insidiously, I am aware of instances in which currently employed people submitted their resume to a contingent recruiter, and that recruiter went around the applicant to their current employer to inform them that their employee was looking for another job and inquired if they were interested in backfill candidates.

In response to these concerns, I suggest the following approach. Consult with your local network for recommendations and introductions to regional/local contingent recruiters. Follow up the e-introduction within a day via email and include your IJP and a request for a fifteen-minute introductory call. Do not send your resume in advance. If they do not agree to a call, then walk away. After having the initial discussion, send them your resume with their acceptance of the stipulation that they cannot share your resume without your prior permission via email.

The same guidelines apply regarding follow-up. For a given job opportunity, ask the recruiter what their relationship with the hiring executive is, if they have a contingent fee agreement with the company, and how many candidates they are sending to the client. The intent of these queries is to understand whether this recruiter can truly assist you with this role or if you are just another resume they are "throwing over the fence." You will also want to ask them at what interval you should reconnect.

As the default, follow up monthly with a brief positive email that reiterates your appreciation of them keeping you in mind for appropriate opportunities. Attach your resume and IJP.

INTERNAL COMPANY RECRUITERS

Types of Roles—The company's internal recruiters can be involved in all open positions.

Their Value Proposition to Companies—Their insider knowledge should enable them to effectively assess cultural fit but not technical skill or experience fit.

Candidates They Seek—I wish I knew. It is very situational. Hopefully, they are acting as an unbiased extension of the hiring executive. Sometimes, under the premise of inclusion, they actively exclude candidates with immutable characteristics that are not on the recruiter's checklist.

How to Originally Connect and Maintain a Relationship with Them—Your first contact with them will be in response to an executive referral, your online application, or from an external recruiter sharing your resume. The recruiter serves a dual role of internal coordinator of the interview schedule and as a negative filter on the selection process. They cannot say "yes" to your candidacy, but they can knock you out of consideration. As a result, tread very carefully when interacting with the internal recruiter.

I suggest you consistently show them deference and act on whatever coaching they provide. They likely have very little knowledge of the decision process and timing, so set your expectations accordingly. I recommend that you use the interview process to develop a direct line of communication with the hiring executive so that you can conduct the follow-up process with them.

CHAPTER 8

OTHER JOB SEARCH AIDS

Now that we have covered the major job search elements, let's look at other job search aides. For this topic, there are two major sources of assistance: LinkedIn and on-line job boards.

LINKEDIN

LinkedIn can be a powerful job search effort multiplier, if it is used correctly. However, the days of "one click apply" are behind you. If you do so, at best you are just feeding your resume into an automated resume review software that is geared to filter out your resume due to too much or too little experience, employment gaps, etc. At worst, you are losing control of your resume to an unscrupulous recruiter who is spreading your resume around the market without your permission or a hacker using your personal information to further their phishing schemes.

However, LinkedIn can be an asset to your job search in three areas:

Vetting Your Ideal Job Profile

When you are developing your IJP and MD, conduct two-phased research. In the first phase, review the LinkedIn profile of the people who currently hold the role you seek in the companies of interest on your MD. The purpose is to identify the core skills and accomplishments of the incumbents in the jobs you are targeting, so you know what to feature in your profile as well as "buzzwords" currently in vogue. In the second phase, conduct a similar review on potential competitors by using a Boolean search to identify people with roles you seek in the geography you are targeting. Since titles do vary between companies for roughly the same role, run several variations. Here is an example for the head of accounting in the Dallas-Fort Worth marketplace:

- VP of Accounting and Dallas-Fort Worth
- Vice President of Accounting and Dallas-Fort Worth
- CAO and Dallas-Fort Worth
- Chief Accounting Officer and Dallas-Fort Worth
- Controller and Dallas-Fort Worth

For each of these iterations, you only need to look at the first two pages of results, as they are the ones recruiters will most likely be contacting. Review their profiles to identify the skills and experiences they have accumulated.

When reviewing the results from these iterations, make an honest assessment on whether your professional background is competitive. Sometimes it may be just a matter of using the current buzzwords. Other times, it may be a skill or experience gap. If your IJP is aspirational, there should be a gap. However, if the gap is substantial or across several skill sets, your ideal job target may be delusional. In that case, you may want to limit the time you pursue this job target before you adjust it to a role for which you are more competitive.

Improve Your Visibility to Recruiters

Most recruiters use LinkedIn to identify candidates for the roles they are trying to fill. Therefore, it is an ideal vehicle to broadcast your IJP and value proposition to the audience you are trying to reach. Although it is essential that it reinforces your messaging (verbatim if possible) from your MD and resume, be cognizant of the current best way to structure your messaging on LinkedIn. Keeping pace with the ever-changing algorithms and best practices of LinkedIn is not my area of expertise. I suggest you invest in a LinkedIn consultant. The best way to find them is to ask your local in-transition networking group for recommendations.

Final thoughts on improving your visibility on LinkedIn. There is an "Open to Finding a New Job" button on your profile. Turn it on. Do not worry that it highlights that you are in a career transition. It amplifies your availability to the recruiters searching for candidates. You do not want to waste your time and energy on firms who only want to interview working professionals. Secondly, update your profile weekly with a brief positive update on your job search or further skill development. This will refresh your name on searches being conducted by recruiters and demonstrate that you are not a "loaf of stale bread on the shelf" but rather a vibrant available candidate.

Effective Way to Build Your Network and Build Market Awareness

I have previously mentioned how LinkedIn can be utilized as a research tool. In this sense, it is the inverse of the previous section, where you were trying to raise your profile via LinkedIn. You are now using the job aid to find people of interest and build your awareness of companies of interest. I expect you will receive training in this area as well when engaging a LinkedIn consultant, but I did want to share two features to assist in your search.

LinkedIn has an option to upgrade to "Premium Career." The cost is nominal on an annual basis. It provides several features, including advanced search capabilities, access to the network's AI capabilities, and, most importantly, access to the InMail™ functionality. This allows you to send an email via LinkedIn to a person who is not a connection to you. This may be the equivalent of a cold approach email, but because users understand that it costs money to send one, people tend to take notice of it and respond.

Join a virtual group within LinkedIn. There is a plethora of groups within LinkedIn that cover the full gamut of interests and shared histories. Some are for alumni of a company or college, others are focused on professional disciplines, and still others are personal passion groups. By joining several groups that are associated with your job search, you will be establishing connection points with people who could potentially assist with your job search. Please note that by joining groups within LinkedIn you will be increasing the traffic on your daily feed, which may "drown out" the updates that may be more central to your job search. In addition, it may expose you to people bombarding you with their own business development approaches. Like everything else, there are trade-offs, so decide what is best for you.

ONLINE JOB BOARDS

Online job boards are similar to some aspects of LinkedIn in that they offer the illusion of a multitude of job opportunities where you can effectively compete. In reality, they are a repository of job listings that range from legitimate to expired or filled to phony and that are simultaneously being viewed by a very large audience. If the job posting is legitimate, it is most certainly going to be inundated with responses, and the company that posted the role will be using software to winnow down the resumes to be reviewed by a human. As we discussed previously, the complex work history of a well-experienced professional does not "score" well in that process, and those candidates are likely to be screened out during the initial filtering process.

Given that these job boards lack the structure and recourse of LinkedIn, I believe they are even more susceptible to recruiters posting stale or filled job leads to fish for resumes for their "inventory" and for scammers to be phishing for personal information that they can use for their other illegal activities. Regardless of the challenges, job boards can serve a limited purpose if you use them correctly. Given the volume of leads and wide distribution, I recommend you review the job board daily, either after 5:00 p.m. or before 7:00 a.m. that way, the time spent on job boards won't interfere with your availability to effectively contact working professionals.

For job postings that appear to score well against your IJP, review your LinkedIn connections for first- and second-level contacts at the target company and hopefully a relevant executive in that firm. Then reach out to the intermediary contact and request a connection to the person in the firm you are targeting. Your note should contain two elements:

- A copy of the job posting along with a brief note as to why you are a solid fit. This will give the intermediary the confidence that the introduction will be well received.
- A draft of the introductory note asking for assistance with applying for the job posting.

You will probably have more success if you ask for a conversation to discuss their perspective on the role and insight into the company rather than direct assistance in the application process.

Once you have your discussion with them, they are likely to help with the application process.

If you do not have a viable LinkedIn connection to the company posting the role, then ignore the posting and focus your time and energy on more productive pursuits. The maxim of success is measured in progress rather than activity is especially true here.

CHAPTER 9

THE JOB INTERVIEW

Now that we have covered the various avenues to gain access to the roles you are targeting, let's move on to a discussion of an effective approach to interviewing.

PHASE 1—PREPARATION

Since an interview is at the top of the Staircase to Success and the goal of all your networking efforts, being well prepared should be obvious, but you would be surprised how many try to "wing it." By conducting the requisite preparation, you will be better informed for the interview and more relaxed, which will allow you to project the "normal" you, instead of the overly stressed version.

The elements of preparation will vary depending upon whether you are interviewing with an external recruiter (in which you may not know the company name) or with an executive at the target company. Regardless, you will want to work through the following steps.

The first step is to score this job description against your IJP. If it does not score highly, then do not take the interview. Save this time and effort to pursue career opportunities that do score well. If you have been in transition for a while, the offer of a job interview is highly seductive as it helps you feel validated and worthwhile as a professional. Stay disciplined, follow the process, and have faith that you will find a job that fits your IJP.

The second step is to develop and practice the core questions you will encounter in almost every interview. The first is: "Why did you leave your last role?" Unless you were escorted out by the police, you probably have a good story to tell. What they are trying to understand is whether there was some type of performance or personality issue in the prior role that is likely to reoccur. The best-structured answer I have ever heard was from a friend of mine who has been a recruiter for many years. The answer has three parts:

The Intro—Make a very positive comment about your prior company. For example: "I really enjoyed my opportunity to be part of the leadership team at Company X, and I am glad I was able to make the contribution to their success that I did."

Reason for Departure—Share a "no-fault" explanation that will allay any concerns they may have about your personality or performance. Here are several examples:

- *The Board elected to bring in a new CEO, and he/she decided to bring in people they had worked with in prior companies.* OR
- *The company has struggled for several years, and as a result, my department/role was eliminated in a major RIF (reduction in force).* OR
- *I was originally hired to implement the Y initiative. The company has had a change in direction. Since the initiative is no longer a priority, I decided to look for an opportunity that would better use my skills and experience.* OR
- *The company is relocating its HQ to X city, and I prefer to stay here.*

Closing Statement—Provide assurance that you left on good terms. For example:

> *"When you are ready to move to the reference stage, I would be glad to introduce you to person A, the CXO of my prior firm."*

Another question to be prepared to answer is, "Walk me through your career path to date." They are not looking for a detailed historiography. The objective is to provide a concise overview of your career path. They are looking for you to explain the logic of your career moves and to put into context how the job you are interviewing for fits into that path. When providing your career history, alert them that you will provide a high-level overview and be glad to drill down in areas of interest to them.

The third step of preparation is research. Public companies are easy to research as they are required to publish a detailed commentary on business results every fiscal quarter and year. Privately held companies are less effusive, but there is still a wealth of information available on its website as well as conducting searches on Google and LinkedIn. The goal is to have a basic knowledge of the business's value proposition, product or service portfolio, and the markets where they operate. Without this information, your questions in the interview are likely to be considered insulting, as you will demonstrate that you did not invest the time to understand the company and ask insightful questions.

In addition to understanding the business, your research should uncover the members of the leadership team, along with their work history. Seek to identify shared LinkedIn connections, common company or industry experience, same alma mater, and having lived in the same city or foreign country. The intent is not to make a "big deal" of the commonalities but rather to slip in the connections during your interview if it fits naturally.

PHASE 2—INTERVIEW

It is important to understand that the interviewer will be making judgments about you long before you answer the first question. This means from the time you pull up to the office you need to assume you are being watched. Here are two quick examples. I was interviewing for a role in another state, for which I rented a car. Apparently, in my nervousness, I failed to turn off the headlights when I parked the car. During the interview, the executive's admin entered the room to ask me if I had parked a car in the visitor section and left my headlights on. I falsely claimed it was not my car since I did not want them to think (know) I could be a bit scatterbrained. They did hire me, and subsequently, when I told my now boss and admin that I had fibbed, they laughed it off, but it was not a risk I was willing to take in the interview.

A more serious example occurred when I was conducting interviews with many candidates on a Saturday for a team I was putting together. My wife, who had experience as a recruiter, acted as our greeter/receptionist. As candidates arrived, she escorted them to a large conference room, gave them something to drink, and chatted them up a bit. Before she would bring in each candidate, she would brief us on her initial impression of them. One of them spent his time in the holding pen reading a *Sports Illustrated* he brought. Clearly, he did not value the interview, and therefore, his candidacy was dead on arrival. A woman was dressed professionally, but her blouse was unbuttoned way too far. You can imagine how that conversation went with my wife. The bottom line is to make sure that you are dressed appropriately for the interview and understand there could be judging eyes upon you as soon as you arrive on site.

Now that you have survived the first impression, let's talk about the interview itself. As you interview for different roles, you will start to see that they tend to be variations on common themes. Before answering a question, it is imperative to pause a second or two to identify the "question within the question." Interviewers do not want data; they want information. For example, when they ask about a recent extended gap in your employment, what they are really trying to discern is if there is a reason that makes you undesirable for employment.

Don't tell them that you were being selective about your next role. That signals that you can be overly picky and difficult to work with. Tell them that after your last role ended, you took the opportunity to help a sick relative (pick one), and that person has fully recovered/died, so you are returning to work. Labor laws do not allow them to ask follow-up questions regarding family illnesses, so this answer safely shuts down this line of questioning. This may sound harsh, and it would be better if you had an actual reason for the employment gap that was benign and did not reflect poorly on your candidacy. However, age discrimination is pervasive, so you need to protect yourself from giving employers a reason to conclude that they should doubt your employability.

Another common question within a question is "Tell me about yourself" or "Walk me through your career." They do not want to hear your detailed biography starting from the third-grade spelling bee. Rather, they want to understand what elements of your prior professional experiences have prepared you for success in the role you are currently pursuing. This is the perfect opportunity to intertwine in your answer some of the commonalities you uncovered in your interview preparation phase.

Another more subtle question is, "Why do you want this job?" Avoid the banal pleasantries of "It's a great company/market leader/always wanted to work here." What they are looking for is if you value the opportunity enough to have done the research on the company to identify business dynamics and initiatives that would draw upon your skills and experiences. A few examples include:

> *"When researching your company, I noted your recent push to expand your sales in Europe. I thought my experience in introducing the products/services of Company X would be very applicable and the kind of challenge in which I excel."*

> *"I read in your 10-K that you recently acquired two small competitors and have plans to acquire additional firms. In my last role, I was heavily involved in realizing the synergies from the post-integration process and would enjoy repeating the challenge."*

> *"I have several friends in the industry, and some have prior experience with your firm. They all remarked that the company culture of valuing A, B, and C is a natural fit for me and will enable me to maximize my contribution to the team."*

Toward the end of the interview, you will likely be given the chance to ask a couple of questions. This is an opportunity to demonstrate to the interviewer that you are invested enough in the role to have done your research. It will enable you to reinforce your candidacy, as well as gain valuable information so you can assess whether you want to continue to pursue the role. Here are some questions you may want to ask:

"Tell me about why you joined this firm and your career path since you arrived?" People like to talk about themselves and their accomplishments. It's human nature. They are likely to appreciate your interest in them, and their answer may provide openings for you to mention commonalities to help build a personal bond.

"Tell me about the characteristics of people who have joined the firm at a senior level and have excelled." Their answer should reveal insight into the corporate culture. If it sounds like "Fight Club," and that is not your style, it is best to drop out of the interview process.

"What do you think are the biggest opportunities or challenges for the firm to reach its objectives or full potential?" In their response, you may identify relevant experiences and accomplishments to share with the interviewer. The additional benefit is that you are demonstrating respect for their opinion.

"Is there anything in my professional background I can clarify that would make you more comfortable to recommend that I move forward in the process?" This question is intended to surface any lingering doubts or potential misunderstandings about your skills, experiences, or interest in the job.

The final step in the interview is to ask them what the next step in the interview process and timing is. This is an incredibly important step as it will tell you a lot about your candidacy and enable you to follow up effectively. If you receive a vague answer, it likely indicates that you are either very early in the process for which they will be meeting several other candidates or you are not a prime candidate. If you do receive a specific timeframe for feedback, that provides you "permission" to follow up at that time. Alternatively, if you do not receive a specific timeframe for feedback, suggest one. Two weeks is a reasonable starting point.

PHASE 3—FOLLOW-UP

The interview is not over until you receive a yes or no on advancing to the next step in the process, so a follow-up process that reinforces your value proposition is key. The process has several phases.

Same Day—Send out a short note expressing appreciation for their time and consideration for the interview, reinforce your candidacy with a key point or two from your conversation with them, confirm your interest in the role, and confirm the date for feedback.

Day After Feedback Day—If they said it would be two weeks before they would be ready to provide feedback, give them the two weeks and a day before you send them a follow-up note. When writing the note, never use the words "following up" because it has the connotation of them owing you something. It would be better to say something like:

> *"Per our conversation, I am circling back/checking in to see if you have feedback on my candidacy for the role, as well as the next steps and timing. I remain quite interested in the role and am looking forward*

to continuing the conversation when you are ready to do so."

If a follow-up day has not been established during the interview, you may want to follow up in a week and adjust your note accordingly.

Continued Follow-Up—Although filling the senior role may be a priority for the firm, the candidate selection process must compete with the individual priorities of each of the members of the selection process. Therefore, you will need to be more patient than you may want to be and maintain a low-pressure, follow-up cadence that reinforces your value proposition rather than reveals your insecurities or weaknesses. If there is no response to your Day After Feedback Day follow-up, then two weeks later, send another brief note. It is important that the note does not sound like you are sitting around waiting for the phone to ring. My recommendation is that you conduct some quick research on the Internet on topics that were discussed during your interview and use it as the basis of your reconnecting note. Here is an example to consider:

> *"Dear [Interviewer Name],*
>
> *I hope your week is going well. I was doing some research and found the attached article. It reminded me of our conversation about X. I trust you are extremely busy with other pressing priorities. I am looking forward to continuing the conversation of my candidacy for the Y role when you are ready to do so."*

The purpose of this note is two-fold. One is to acknowledge that they are dealing with many competing priorities and that you are quite comfortable working within their timetable. Secondly, remind them of the strong qualities you would bring to the business. Repeat this two-week cadence with different articles for a couple of iterations. At some point, you can add a request to "set your expectations" on when they would have feedback. After three or four follow-ups, accept the uncomfortable truth that either the company is not moving forward with filling the role currently or at least they are not moving forward with your candidacy. Resist the urge to go away angry or frustrated, and remind yourself that when you were hiring people for your team, the process was one of stops and starts.

Send a final note that reiterates your interest in the role and indicates that you will not be sending future notes. However, you would be glad to pick up the conversation if and when they are ready to do so.

CHAPTER 10

JOB OFFER NEGOTIATION

PHASE 1—PREPARATION

Now that you worked the interview process to perfection, it's time to move on to the job offer negotiation. All your hard work has finally culminated into an offer! Naturally, this will be a time of excitement and anxiety. Tread carefully to choreograph a negotiation that maximizes the job offer; it starts with preparation.

Print out your IJP. Rank the elements in importance, either numerically or in categories of most important, very important, or important. Annotate ideal and minimum acceptable parameters for each element. For example, based on your financial situation, compensation may be the most important factor. You'll have your ideal number, which is usually not their offer, and then the low number, which is the minimum you'll consider until you walk away from the opportunity. Another example could be job location. This may be your second highest criterion, and you may be hoping for complete flexibility but require at least one day of work from home per week.

The next step is to identify which elements were discussed during the interview process to your satisfaction. At this time, review your notes to confirm you have clarity on the obvious elements of compensation structure and amounts, what departments report into this role, to whom this role reports, as well as the location and/or amount of travel expected.

Some people may advocate that this is a game of manipulation or the time to "play hardball." I recommend the opposite. This is the time to be open and honest in your communication and keep an open mind to the hiring company's point of view. This company will be your professional home for the next few years, so it is imperative to create a foundation of trust and respect.

PHASE 2—VERBAL / PRE-OFFER DISCUSSION

Normally, you will be contacted by the recruiter or the hiring executive with the good news that they will be making a job offer before you receive it in writing. This is an ideal time to understand their offer and hopefully negotiate better terms before it is solidified in writing. Ask the company representative to walk through the offer's various elements and make notes on your IJP pages. At this time, do not agree, disagree, or ask for the rationale for the values they are sharing. The key is to allow them to do a complete download in a low-pressure environment.

Once they have finished, quickly identify the gaps to your IJP and their relative importance.

When is it your time to talk, begin the conversation by thanking them for sharing a *draft* of the offer and that you are very excited about joining the firm. Do not use language indicating you are accepting the offer as is or are countering the offer (which is a form of rejecting it). Let them know you want to better understand the offer and the rationale behind it.

Start with confirming the elements of your IJP that were previously discussed and agreed upon but not mentioned in today's verbal offer. This may seem like a waste of time, but it is not. During the interview process, you talked with several people, and although you may have received an acceptable answer from an interviewer, it does not ensure that it is part of your final job offer. Examples of this may include how many days a week or month you will need to be in an office. This is a critical point if you live in another city from the office. In the same vein, what travel and or temporary living expenses will the firm pay, and for how long?

You will also want to confirm to whom you will report in the organization and what departments will report to your role. I know of a CIO who was interviewing for another CIO role. During the extended process, the company went through a restructuring, and the CIO role would now report to the CFO instead of the CEO. When that realization was uncovered during the discussion of the verbal offer, the candidate shared that the change in reporting structure was a deal breaker and that they would walk away. The firm relented.

Please note that if your verbal offer includes (or the response to any of your clarifying questions includes) a reference to standard company policies, you need to ask for a copy of those policies before you can accept the offer. Their version of "standard" could be quite different from your expectations. This can be particularly true around company benefit costs and coverage.

Once you have aligned and confirmed with the employer on the relatively undisputed elements, ask them their rationale for the job element(s) that are out of range from your perspective. It is imperative that you actively listen to their response. There may be indications of structural impediments such as compensation band limits for the role or limited amount of equity available. They may disclose that a gap between your skills and experiences to the perfect profile they were seeking is the driver for a lower compensation offer. If it is the former, then it will be difficult to move them. If it is the latter, share with them that, based on your local market intelligence, the market for your skills is within the range you shared with them. This intelligence can be based on peers in similar roles or on the other roles for which you have recently been asked to interview. After sharing your perspective, inquire if there is flexibility in their number. As a fallback, ask if it is possible to have a salary review after six and twelve months or if a minimum bonus payout can be assured.

As a case in point, when I was interviewing for my most recent sales leader role, throughout the process I had several conversations with human resources regarding compensation expectations. My minimum acceptable base salary was fifty percent higher than what they were targeting to pay. She explained that the offer was what they normally pay new hires for the role. My calm rebuttal was that I do not have the typical skill and experience profile of their new hires and that my perception of my market value was confirmed by the other roles for which I was actively interviewing. In the end, they made an offer at the bottom of my acceptable range but with a higher sales target than I had anticipated. When I asked them if my quota was higher due to my higher base salary, they said, "Yes." I responded, "Sounds fair." Receiving a direct and honest response to my direct question was a great way to start with a foundation of trust.

The last element to discuss, because it can be contentious, is the topic of severance. It is an inherently negative topic, akin to a prenuptial agreement, but just as important. This becomes even more important if the compensation elements fall short of your goals. I recommend you frame the discussion as a natural consequence of the role for which you are being hired. The company is looking for you to complete a strategic imperative. Once that is resolved, the firm will have a different imperative. You may or may not have the ideal skill set for the next imperative, so the firm may elect to replace you. Given that firms are very selective at this level, there is an extended period for job search and interviewing, so you want to ensure your family is protected. I suggest you ask for twelve months' salary plus full company health benefits and settle for a minimum of six months if you must do so.

At the end, you need to summarize the discussion and conclude on a positive tone. On several occasions, I have used the following approach:

> *"I really appreciate our open conversation today and you taking my suggested edits into consideration when finalizing the job offer. Please note, I trust your judgment, so I am looking forward to the written offer and will accept it."*

The intention of this closing statement is to let them know that you value the opportunity, respect their position, and are giving them a chance to be magnanimous—an offer that is hard for them to refuse. By letting them know there will not be multiple rounds of negotiation, you encourage them to go through the approval process to amend your offer letter. Within an hour of your offer negotiation, follow up with an email summary of your conversation that reiterates your spoken summary of the job offer elements and details the suggested changes to the verbal offer.

As a side note, if you have been interviewing with other firms, give them a heads-up that you are expecting an offer from another firm but that they are your preferred career opportunity. Let them know you can delay your start by two weeks to provide a better offer.

PHASE 3—ACCEPTANCE OF THE WRITTEN OFFER

Assuming the company has incorporated some of your requested changes from the verbal discussion, you have obligated yourself to accept it. I suggest you request a start date two weeks out. Use the time to relax, enjoy the fact that you have a new job on the near horizon, and maybe take a family trip, as it will be a while before you will be able to do so.

If the other firm comes through with a better job offer during this intervening period, you are free to take it. No doubt, this will irreparably damage your relationship with the firm, the executive team, and the recruiter, but the reality is that companies act in their own self-interest, so you might as well do the same. My father worked in human resources at a very large company for four decades and once remarked that of the thousands of people he hired, twenty-five percent never showed up for the first day of work, and the firm wishes that another twenty-five percent never did!

If you think landing your ideal job means that you are finished with this process, you are mistaken. Your networking efforts must continue.

CHAPTER 11

WHAT'S NEXT?

Congratulations on landing a job scoring highly on your IJP! As heady as this event is, an important question remains: What do you do next? Since networking does not come naturally to most people, there is a tendency to stop it and bury oneself in the new role. On one level, this approach is understandable, however, your recent challenge to find this new role should confirm the importance of ensuring you never again need to commence a job search from a "cold start." The notion that the new job will last the rest of your career is seductive, but the reality is your needs, and those of companies continue to evolve, so you will likely need to repeat the job search process sooner than you think.

Now that you are employed, your approach will pivot from job search to classic networking. There are subtle differences, but you will find the latter to be less intrusive, more pleasurable, and easier to sustain. You are no longer asking for the favor of introductions, job search assistance, or interviewing for roles. Your focus now is on deepening the relationships you initiated during your job search and continuing to grow your network at a relaxed pace. This is essential as your recently expanded network was introduced to you as an unemployed executive, sharing your work experience in the hope that they would assist in your job search. By continuing to interact (network) with them, your conversations are now about work issues you are resolving in your current role, as well as granting networking favors to them and their contacts. You have transformed your public image from needy to successful.

There are two sides to the sustained networking effort: internal and external. The internal side refers to the networking effort within your new company. The external one refers to the people you met during your recent job search. The activities are quite different, so let's look at them in turn.

The three main goals of your internal networking are to rapidly increase your understanding of the company's challenges and opportunities, as well as how the various departments interact with each other, and develop personal relationships throughout the organization; by accomplishing the first two objectives, you will greatly increase the probability that you will successfully integrate into your new role and company.

There is a whole genre of books regarding "The First 100 Days" work plans. I have not read any, so I am unable to make a recommendation. I can, however, share with you the internal networking approach I have used on several occasions. I conducted it in phases.

Phase One is focused on peers to the role I just accepted. I set up an offsite introductory discussion over coffee, breakfast, or lunch. I suggest an offsite location because it is a neutral location that de-emphasizes any power dynamic between the two roles. During this conversation, seek to build a personal connection with the other business leader by sharing information about your personal life and taking a sincere interest in theirs.

There are also several business-related questions you may want to ask them, including:

- *Tell me about your time here at the firm and the changes you have seen.*
- *What do you think are the biggest opportunities or challenges facing the business?*
- *In your experience, tell me about the characteristics of the people who have thrived since joining the firm.*
- *How should our two departments interact to ensure maximum performance against the company's goals?*
- *Who are the key people on your team that I should get to know?*
- *What coaching or insight can you share on how I should best interact with our common boss? If you both are below the C-suite level and do not share the same boss, then this question should be about their boss, who is part of the C-suite.*

The intent of these discussions is to create a foundation for a relationship before there is any of the normal friction between business functions. You accomplish this by showing respect and some deference to their opinion, based on their experience at the firm, without establishing a subservient dynamic.

Phase Two is focused on the key direct reports identified during your discussion with peers in Phase One. Send them an email requesting time for a brief, introductory conversation, as their boss suggested that they are someone you should know better. Offer to do this before work or in their office—anywhere but your office. There is no need to exert your hierarchy; your role has already been established. Ask them the first four questions above that you asked their boss. The goal is to demonstrate that you value them as a person and contributor to the business's success and that they feel comfortable having a work conversation with you. The positive relationship you build with them will likely extend to the subordinates on your team.

Phase Three is to meet with your boss and provide a concise summary of what you have learned during your "listening tour." Hopefully, they will provide some feedback and some context to what you have heard. At the very least, it will clearly demonstrate that you are making a focused effort to understand the business and the people so you can become a highly successful addition to the leadership team.

There is no final phase because your internal networking effort never ends. Periodically, you will need to reconnect with the same people to repair and strengthen the bonds that fray over time from the normal friction of business.

The external networking effort seems to be more of a challenge for people. I have seen too many people claim they are too busy with their new role, such that they stop attending networking events and become unresponsive to emails until they are conducting their next job search. That approach is incredibly damaging to your prospects of gaining the support of others in the future. By pulling a disappearing act, you are demonstrating to others that you do not understand the importance of reciprocity and consider networking as a one-way flow of benefit to you. People who aided you the first time you contacted them did so with the understanding that, at some point, each of us needs help. By demonstrating your selfishness, you will have forfeited those sources of assistance for your future searches.

This effort has a variety of elements. For your closest circle of job search supporters and advisers and those who provided the job lead or assisted in the process, send them an email the day after you accept the new role. Share your appreciation for their support and let them know you will circle back four weeks after your start date to set up a call or coffee time to debrief on your first month and to catch up with them. You absolutely need to make good on your offer to follow up to set up the reconnect session. These folks invested time, energy, and their own networking capital to assist you in your search. Show them the respect they have earned.

If a professional service provider was instrumental in your search, assist them in making a business connection to your new firm. I am not talking about handing them an engagement without regard to cost or qualifications. Rather, provide them insight into the business issues that are relevant to their services and invite them to be one of the competitors for service opportunities. If the private equity backers of the firm have directed that certain service providers be used for certain services, explain that to the connection and look for secondary and tertiary service opportunities. If your service provider connection provides services for another corporate function, broker a meeting with the appropriate business leader in the firm. Whether it results in business or not for the service provider, you will have demonstrated a sincere act of reciprocity, enabling you to maintain this valuable connection.

This may seem too transactional or "quid pro quo," but it is not. It is an honest assessment of how service providers operate. Their continued survival is predicated on their ability to gain new business as there is a natural attrition on their existing business base. They encounter a finite number of job leads and must be judicious regarding whom they introduce into their network of friends. Therefore, they need to focus their support on the business leaders who will be reciprocal now or in the not-too-distant future.

After you have connected with your immediate circle of supporters, update your LinkedIn profile to reflect that you successfully landed a new role. No doubt you will be inundated with well wishes. Do your best to send a short thank-you acknowledgment. Periodically, send out an update via LinkedIn on your latest successful initiative. This will reinforce that you are a thriving professional to a broad audience.

It is important that you continue to attend the networking groups you participated in during your job search. You are no longer seeking the assistance of others, so you can be more relaxed in your approach and enjoy your conversations with the other members. As your conversations are now about business issues, you will transform your image within the group from job seeker to accomplished business leader yet stay top of mind if another great career opportunity arises.

The final phase, if there is one, is to help others in their job search. Undoubtedly, you benefited from the kindness of others in your own recent job search. Create the world you want to live in.

ABOUT THE AUTHOR

John Hughes has been the Director of Business Development at BDO USA, the fifth-largest global accounting, tax, and advisory firm for the last seven years. His prior roles in Dallas include Manager of Business Development at Wilson Perumal & Company, Head of Field Finance for FleetPride, and the Director of Finance-Operations & Supply Chain at Hostess Brands.

His prior professional experience includes Vice President of Financial Planning at Musician's Friend in Oregon, M&A and valuation projects in Latin America, as well as various financial leadership roles at IBM, The Coca-Cola Company, and Aramark. He leads the Ambassador Program in the Dallas FEI chapter.

John's career coaching experience includes leading BDO's Friend of the Firm Job Search Boot Camp and leading the Atlanta Chapter of FENG for three years, during which he led career search discussions twice a month. Since 2018, he has led BDO's Friend of the Firm job search assistance program. Through these presentations and three progressively shorter career transitions, he developed the ***Five Essential Elements of a Successful Job Search*** process.

He utilized this process to move to Dallas without knowing anyone. How effective was it?

- Within four months, it resulted in a one-month project.
- Six months later, it resulted in a multi-year role.
- Years later, it facilitated a change in careers within two months.
- The last transition was ten weeks and resulted in offers in two different industries and roles.

John has an MBA in International Management and Finance from the Irish Management Institute in Dublin (with Fordham University), a Certificate in Strategic Leadership from Penn State, and a BS in Business Management from Le Moyne College in upstate New York. John currently resides in Florida and has been happily married for longer than he can remember and certainly longer than he deserves.

JohnPatrickHughes.com

ACKNOWLEDGMENTS

I would like to acknowledge the significant contribution of Caroline Hughes in the writing of this book. Her astute editing skills and ability to act as a sounding board for material unfamiliar to her were essential to translating twenty-plus years of experiences and anecdotes into a cogent and coherent guidebook.

Secondly, I would like to acknowledge my parents, who gifted me with a hyper-analytical brain and taught me the value of unwavering perseverance.

Finally, to all the people and companies that hired me, promoted me, and fired me, thank you for unwittingly playing your part in creating the experiences that are the basis of this book.

WORK WITH JOHN

Are you in transition and looking to accelerate the timeline to your next job offer?

John offers one-on-one executive coaching to a select number of candidates a year. His services include a personal review of your IJP, MD, resume, and other key elements vital to the job search and offer process. Working with John will provide you with the confidence, clarity, and strategic plan of action to help you secure your next role.

To schedule a consultation, email his office at
admin@JohnPatrickHughes.com.

Made in the USA
Columbia, SC
09 February 2025

53062813R00093